D0502038

I've Got
99 Swing Thoughts, but "Hit the Ball" Ain't One

O O O

I've Got
99 Swing Thoughts, but "Hit the Ball" Ain't One

PICK UP THE PACE TO PICK UP YOUR GAME

o o o

Christopher Smith
with Steve Eubanks

Crown Publishers
New York

Copyright © 2007 by Christopher Smith

All rights reserved.
Published in the United States by Crown Publishers, an imprint of the Crown
Publishing Group, a division of Random House, Inc., New York.
www.crownpublishing.com

Crown is a trademark and the Crown colophon is a registered trademark
of Random House, Inc.

Library of Congress Cataloging-in-Publication Data

Smith, Christopher, 1963 Apr. 24–
I've got 99 swing thoughts, but "hit the ball" ain't one / Christopher Smith;
with Steve Eubanks.—1st ed.
Includes index.
1. Golf—Study and teaching.   I. Eubanks, Steve, 1962–   II. Title.
GV965.S616 2007
796.352—dc22   2007020751

ISBN 978-0-307-38114-9

Printed in the United States of America

Design by Joseph Rutt

10 9 8 7 6 5 4 3 2 1

First Edition

Nothing divides one so much as thought.
—R. H. BLYTH

Contents

○ ○ ○

I've Got
99 Swing Thoughts,
but "Hit the Ball"
Ain't One

o o o

Introduction

O   O   O

"Welcome to My (and Every Other Golfer's) Nightmare"

John Daly was playing golf in California with shock-rock legend Alice Cooper (you know, "Welcome to My Nightmare," "No More Mr. Nice Guy," "School's Out"?). Alice is a jolly golfer, someone who tucks his shoulder-length hair under a cap and plays a very respectable game. He also offers commentary on every shot you or anyone else in the group hits. Hit a tee shot left and Alice will say, "Thurman Munson, baby: that was a dead yank." Or chunk one in the right bunker and he'll say, "Rush Limbaugh: fat and right." He is delightful to play with, and one of the great storytellers on the celebrity pro-am circuit. But playing with J.D. caused Alice some problems. John played so fast, he didn't give Alice an opportunity to comment on the shots. Alice would hit a high, spinning wedge and say, "That's gonna suck like the last *Matrix* movie," only to realize that he had talked during John's swing.

Putting was especially tough. Just about the time Alice was ready to say, "Hey, John, what do you think this one's going to do?" J.D. was rolling a twenty-footer in for birdie. John takes about three seconds to line up his putts and another three to set up and make his stroke. He also ranks among the best in the world at making putts inside twenty feet. John is still the only player to lead the Tour in both driving distance and par saves.

After three holes of talking over his partner, Alice said, "John, why do you play so fast? Don't you ever line up a shot?"

"I line all of them up."

"What are you talking about? You hit it so fast."

John put an arm on Alice's shoulder and nodded toward a radio tower in the distance. "You see that tower out there?"

"Sure," Alice said.

"Okay, point your finger at that tower."

Alice did.

"Good. Now, I want you to take your time and aim your finger at the tower. Take as much time as you need and get your finger as close to the line as you can."

Alice closed one eye, straightened his arm, took his time, and aimed a finger at the tower.

"Do you think you got closer to the line by taking all that extra time?"

"Probably not," Alice admitted.

"You got closer when you just pointed," John said. "When you take all that time lining up and aiming, you talk yourself out of your first instinct, which is usually dead-on. You'll hit it a lot closer to the hole and make a lot more putts if you take one look and pull the trigger. Don't aim; just point and go."

John was exactly right. Most people who line up three-foot putts from every angle, who examine the contours of the green when their ball is ninety yards away, or who spend inordinate amounts of time aiming their feet, hips, shoulders, hands, and clubface make no more putts and hit the ball no closer to the hole than the person who looks at the target one time, sets up, and swings. In fact, people who look and fire usually play better, because they haven't overanalyzed the situation and talked themselves out of simply reacting to the target.

Golf, unlike many sports, gives you plenty of time to think about what you're doing. The ball sits still on the ground, waiting, taunting: "Go on, hit me; hit me hard. Take your time. The spotlight's on you. Check your grip, tighten up those hands, get those clumsy clown feet pointed in the right direction, weight distributed just so—plenty of time—hitch your pants like that guy on television; wave the clubhead back and forth over me a second or two. Scowl. Now, swing!"

When Hall of Fame running back Marcus Allen was first learning to play golf, he heard the ball's trash talk. Watching Marcus listen to the voices in his head was like watching a pilot go through a preflight checklist—club gripped with the last three fingers of the left hand, check; right hand on top, check; weight on the balls of the feet, check; spine angle tilted to the right, check; upper body tilted from the waist, left arm straight, chin high, ball played off the left heel, check, check, check. And on and on.

During one round, Marcus became so frustrated after whiffing a shot in the fairway that he threw his 5-iron fifty yards downrange, turned to his instructor, threw up his hands, and said, "I'm an athlete! I've got a Heisman Trophy, an NFL MVP award, a Super Bowl ring, a bust in the Hall of Fame. I can still throw a baseball seventy miles an hour. But I can't hit a ball that's sitting on the ground!"

Golf can turn a skilled professional athlete into a fit-pitching basket case. But Marcus shouldn't feel isolated or alone in his frustration. The mental machinations he went through and the frustration he felt from the lack of a decent result are more common than most people realize. Even great golfers fall victim to the ball's acerbic lyrics—"Hit me / Smack me / Beat me, now / Choke that grip / Wrinkle your brow."

Greg Norman entered the final round of the 1996 Masters with a six-shot lead and appeared unbeatable. He had led after every round and was hitting the ball great. But on Sunday Greg experienced one of the greatest collapses in major championship history.

A lot of experts have analyzed Greg's swing and attempted to explain what happened that fateful afternoon. Throughout the week, and even through the opening holes on Sunday, Greg took twelve to thirteen seconds to hit every shot. From the time he started his preshot ritual, Greg's routine varied by only one second all week. Then something changed. By the fourth hole of the final round, he was taking seventeen seconds to hit every shot. When he made the turn, he was taking twenty seconds on each shot, and by the time he left Amen Corner he was up to almost thirty seconds. The longer Greg stood over the ball, the more his critical thinking interfered with his ability to execute the shot at hand. I mean, really, how long could you stand over a ball and not think—about anything? As Greg took more and more time, his game went downhill.

The simple fact is, the more swing thoughts you have, the more paralyzed you become, and the less likely you are to hit good golf shots. Your brain also slows down your round. If every thought takes three seconds to process (and that's being generous), then ten swing thoughts add thirty seconds per shot to your round. Twenty swing thoughts add a full minute. For a player who shoots in the 90s, that's an extra hour and a half per round. Suddenly a three-and-a-half-hour round has been stretched to five excruciating hours. Throw in a couple of practice swings for every shot—which are normally infested with swing thoughts themselves—and welcome to the six-hour round of golf.

It takes a long time to process the 99 swing thoughts you bring with you to the tee, but at least you'll be miserable while doing it. Consider one of the basic fundamentals of executing a motor skill—if you have to "think about" how to perform it (the golf swing, for example) during the act, it (the thinking) destroys your ability to perform. Where does that concept leave all your precious swing thoughts? Answer: in the garbage. Having coached thousands of golfers in my career, I have discovered an inverse relationship between the number of swing thoughts you bring to the course and the number of strokes it takes you to finish. With one swing thought it will take you three seconds to hit each shot (John Daly speed) and you will play better, because your mind won't get in the way of your body's ability to execute.

When you play faster and turn off your brain, you shoot lower scores. I should know: in addition to being nominated as one of *Golf Magazine*'s top 100 teachers in the country in 2006, I'm one of the top-ranked speed golfers in the world. In my favorite form of competition (speed golf), your score is the number of shots you take added to the amount of time it takes you to finish the

Hit and run. Christopher in the midst of a round of speed golf.

round, running. If you shoot an 80 in three hours, your speed-golf score is 260.00 (80 shots plus 180 minutes). I do a good bit better than that. In 2005 I set a world speed-golf record at the Chicago Speed Golf Classic by shooting 65 in forty-four minutes and six seconds carrying only six golf clubs.

And ironically, my lowest score ever on the Ghost Creek golf course at Pumpkin Ridge GC (a 6,500-yard layout that hosted the 1993 and 1994 Nike Tour Championships), where I have coached and taught for over eight years, came during a round of speed golf: a five-under-par 66 in forty-eight and a half minutes, again using only six clubs.

To most people this sounds crazy. Okay, regardless of how many strokes you take, you have to be a pretty fit athlete to play eighteen holes of golf in around forty-five minutes on foot, but that's not the point. Most of the students I coach couldn't run from the driving range to the parking lot without stopping for a breather. And I'm not suggesting that to become a better golfer you have to become a marathon runner. What I am saying is that if you play faster, not giving yourself time to second-guess your first impressions, you will play better.

The mind-set of speed golfers is to make quick decisions, go with their gut, and get on with the game. Whether I'm playing speed golf or a casual round with a student, I get to my ball, see the shot in my mind, and execute. No laborious analysis, no pacing around trying to figure the wind direction at every point during the trajectory of my intended shot, and no thoughts of swing mechanics: I look once, waggle the club once, and swing: ready—aim—fire; one—two—three.

Most golfers incorporate at least one and usually several "think" components into that sequence. They get to their ball, and then spend some time thinking; see the shot, and then think . . . and think . . . and think . . . and think some more—"How's your grip? Make sure you keep your arm straight going back. Turn those shoulders as far as you can. Hinge the wrists. Lag the club on the downswing." Only after wasting an inordinate amount of time tying themselves into mental knots do these players finally hit the ball—poorly. As stated by my buddy Dr. Craig Farnsworth, a world-renowned vision and concentration specialist who has worked with superior performers from Nick Faldo to members of the U.S. Navy SEALs teams, "You can't think and act at the same time."

Don't get me wrong: setup and swing technique are important factors in getting the ball from point A to point B. But these skills must be mastered before arriving on the golf course to play. Once the game has begun, it's too late to be learning the swing.

A learned skill is frequently defined as the ability to do something most of the time without thinking about how to do it. You can't do it every time, because you're human. And you don't "forget" a motor skill, like riding a bike or tying your shoe, once you've learned it. If you can't do it competently and unconsciously most of the time, it's not that you have forgotten the motor skill—you simply haven't *learned* it yet.

And yes, learning takes time. That is the golden rule of motor-skill acquisition. Every expert in the motor-learning community agrees with that fact, even though it is contrary to so much of what goes on in the rest of our lives. (The foremost "learners" in the world are kids, who always seem to have *more time* than adults.) Frustration in golfers often comes from not understanding how much time it takes to acquire a new motor skill. We falsely believe that because our computers, phones, stereos, cars, televisions, and everything else in life get the job done so much faster than years before—and because you can pretty much get or do anything now in Western society—we ought to be able to pick up this golf swing thing in a thirty-minute sitcom time frame. Unfortunately, our body and psyche are not computer chips.

Then, once we have acquired the new and more efficient way

to hit the ball, there's the tiny issue of playing the game of golf. Now, that's a whole other ball of wax, and one that takes an abundance of time to understand and address the multitude of mental and physical challenges a golf course presents. To quote the distinguished instructor and coach John Jacobs, "Hitting a golf ball is relatively easy, playing golf is hugely difficult."

Think of a round of golf as being like taking a test: the research, studying, and homework must be done prior to the exam. Once the clock starts on the test, it's too late to study. The test is about demonstrating and performing the skills you've learned ahead of time. The same is true in a round of golf. Once you put the peg in the ground on the first tee, it's time to demonstrate the skills and preparedness you brought with you that day. It's too late to do the homework once the test has begun.

"You gotta dance with who you brung," the great Sam Snead used to say. Unfortunately, too many golfers have not done their homework before arriving at the first hole, so they try to learn and implement those things while they are playing. That is where your 99 swing thoughts come in. You wouldn't feel comfortable getting in an airplane with someone who was still learning to fly, but that is what you're doing to yourself when you show up on the golf course unprepared.

Not only do golfers who try to wing it through the golf test shoot higher numbers with fourteen clubs than I do with six, I can be finished with my round and enjoying a cold beer in the clubhouse before they reach the fourth tee.

TURNING OFF YOUR CONSCIOUS BRAIN

I believe that the biggest impediment to making good golf swings is the conscious human brain, at least that portion of the brain devoted to methodical reasoning, critical analysis, and the scientific method. Although the conscious mind is extremely vital in preparing to hit a golf shot and gathering information after, the actual motion of the golf swing must be performed on autopilot. This seems counterintuitive. After all, we've been told for decades that Jack Nicklaus won eighteen professional majors by "outthinking" his opponents, and Tiger Woods is praised for his ability to concentrate better than most of his opponents. But I contend that Jack, Tiger, Arnold Palmer, Ben Hogan, Ernie Els, and every other great golfer of this or any other generation achieved greatness by knowing when to use their critical faculties and when to turn the light switch off and react: to let the sections of the brain that allow our lungs to breathe, our hearts to beat, and our fingernails to scratch that pesky itch to take over and allow the body to perform in order to hit the desired shot.

I'm not alone in this theory. Motor-skill experts have drawn similar conclusions. Dr. Christian Marquardt, a motor-learning specialist and developer/inventor of the Science and Motion Putt Lab, says, "In order to become proficient, you have to think about nothing while executing a motion, but you should have a supporting mental picture, a 'feel' of the motion. To better understand this, have a look at other motor skills like playing the piano. What is the brain of a skilled pianist thinking while playing? Nothing. The player is feeling the music. The hands are moving automatically in response to what the person feels. The player would not even know how to move his ten fingers in such complex movement patterns."

Ernest Jones echoed those thoughts many years ago in his famed book *Swing the Clubhead*. Said Jones, "You must rid yourself of the distractions of trying to think about all those things against which most golfers are warned. You do not have the time in the fraction of a second between taking the club back and returning it to contact with the ball." A hundred and twenty years ago, Sir Walter Simpson shared many of the same beliefs in his classic book *The Art of Golf*. "There is, I repeat, a categorical imperative in golf—'Hit the Ball.' As soon as any point of style is allowed, during the shot, to occupy the mind more than hitting the ball, a miss, more or less complete, will result," Simpson wrote.

Shinichi Suzuki understood this when he developed the Suzuki method of learning music in the latter half of the twentieth century. Dr. Suzuki knew that young students could never comprehend the complexities of classical music, but children as young as three could feel music and replicate the actions of others to reproduce that feeling. The result was a revolution in music education.

I believe that same kind of revolution is possible in golf, which, like learning classical piano, is little more than a series of complex repetitive movements. Unfortunately, most golf instructors "process teach" the game; that is, they tell the students what motions to make and what thoughts they need to incorporate into their games to make those motions. As a result, golfers stand over the ball forever, going through seemingly endless mental checklists, none of which have anything to do with the feel of your golf swing or with getting the ball in the hole.

Plus, if the information a golf instructor gives you doesn't click with the way you best learn, the instructor might as well be speaking in Farsi. Everyone has an optimal way to set up, swing, and play the game from a strategic standpoint. If the instruction you receive doesn't mesh with how you learn, you and the instructor are wasting time.

The great players throughout history adapted their games to fit their strengths. That is why the best ball strikers of all time—Ben Hogan, Lee Trevino, Moe Norman, Nick Price, Tiger Woods, Byron Nelson—have very different golf swings. Unfortunately, if Ben Hogan were standing on the lesson tee today, most instructors would tell him he needed to get his plane more upright and work his hands less through the hitting area. Trevino would be told to correct his alignment and work on releasing the golf club more efficiently; Byron Nelson would hear that he needed to get the dip out of his downswing; and Moe Norman's swing would require the ten-lesson overhaul package. Thankfully, these players adapted their natural skills and their personal learning models to their golf games. They learned the way that was best for them and swung the club in a way that worked.

Now, think about the actions you perform instinctively. For example, think about how many songs you know by heart. Driving in to work you probably sang a dozen or more as they came on the radio without missing a lyric. Now, how many countries and capitals can you name off the top of your head? Liechtenstein? Khartoum? Did you get those?

And how about the motor-skill act of driving itself: while singing those songs this morning, did you think about how much pressure to apply to the accelerator to keep up with the car ahead of you? Did you think about which muscles you use to apply the brake? How much time did you spend contemplating the motion needed to turn the steering wheel?

On a simpler note, think about every calculation that goes into picking up a glass of water. Your brain has to recognize the glass as something you can, indeed, pick up; then you have to calculate how to move the arm to the glass—which muscles to activate and the precise angle of approach; and then you have to dock the hand with the glass, slowing the approach so as not to knock the item over, opening the hand and then closing it with exactly the right grip pressure to lift the object, but not so much that you break the glass; and finally, you have to lift the glass to your mouth without spilling the contents, motions that would require a bank of computers several seconds to calculate. Yet you can pick up a glass of water while singing a song or reading this book.

That is because learning by feel activates different neurons than learning by logic and rote does. I believe that too many of the thoughts we have always used to learn a golf swing actually retard your body's ability to feel and react to the environment around you. We best learn motor skills by simply doing them—repetition. Through the trial-and-error process and observing and sensing the feedback that comes from the varied results, feel and skill are developed. Again, according to Dr. Marquardt, "Teaching is creating an *external* model for the student, but motor learning is establishing an *internal* model. If the teaching does not match the internal model, it will fail, hence the need for both student and teacher to become more of a coach to facilitate the learning process. You don't teach a child to walk by explaining the motions of putting one foot in front of the other; you hold the child up during a few practice runs, and then you let him fall a few times as he learns the feel of walking on his own."

As an example of how this applies to golf, think of the Bob Dylan song that says, "You don't need a weatherman to know which way the wind blows." Political metaphors aside, old Bob was right. Just step outside and you instinctively know whether the breeze is in your face, at your back, or cutting across from left or right. A million years of evolution have honed humans' ability to figure out wind direction without any complicated analysis. If the tops of the trees are waving to the left, you instinctively know that the wind is blowing from right to left; you don't need to conduct a series of controlled double-blind experiments to figure it out.

Golfers let dozens of unnecessary thoughts cloud what our subconscious knows instinctively. I've seen countless players stand on the first tee and think, "Okay, do I hit my driver here? What if I snap hook it like I was doing on the practice tee? Will the rough stop it before it goes out of bounds? Is my right-hand grip too strong? Do I have the ball teed up the correct height? Where am I aligned? How much weight is on my right foot? How about my spine angle? Am I bent enough from the waist? Too much? How do I look? How's my waggle? Now, make sure to get good extension on your takeaway. Okay, swing!"

After this golfer misses the shot, he pounds his driver into the ground and says, "Shoot, I forgot about the wind."

Forgot about the wind! The wind is the one thing this golfer couldn't forget: the thing that we've been able to feel and judge instinctively since our ancestors were hunting with stone axes. In order to forget about the wind, this guy's mind had to be so cluttered with useless data that his brain hit overload. He forgot about the one thing he shouldn't have had to think about at all.

Overthinking is the number-one killer of good golf scores. Sam Snead was once asked what he was thinking about as he swung a driver. Never one for meaningless pontification, Snead said, "Nothing. You can't think and swing at the same time, and if you do, the ball ain't going where you want it to."

Snead's quip is true of all sports, but his follow-up was even more telling. When asked what it was like to play great golf, Sam said, "It's like dark blue water, all oily and calm." Does that sound like a process thought to you? Sam didn't realize it at the time, but he was using mental pictures, colors, and feel when he played well. And as he said, he wasn't thinking about anything.

Unfortunately, it is my belief that we have been programmed in both our practice and playing habits to use conscious swing thoughts. The goal in the pages that follow is to exorcise those thoughts and replace them with pictures, feel, and tasks that will help you to better strike the ball and shoot lower scores—without running between shots.

In talking with the handful of great golfers who have shot 59 in competition, one thing stands out: every one of them, from Al Geiberger to Annika Sörenstam, says that every moment in the magical round had a rhythm, almost like a march or the steady beat of a four-four piece of music. No one was providing a backbeat on the course, obviously, but each of these players felt in sync during their walks, talks, swings, and putts throughout the round. And none of them can name one mechanical swing thought that entered their minds that day.

IT'S JUST LIKE SIGNING YOUR NAME

If I hand someone a baseball and say, "Throw this ball at that tree," he or she has no trouble following my instructions. The pupil looks at the tree and throws. Not one person in my close to twenty years as an instructor has taken a practice throw without the ball, then waggled his arm back and forth to figure out how far to reach back. They don't stand there endlessly and motionless, staring at the tree as if hypnotized by its bark. No one has considered how far back to bring the arm or how much shoulder rotation is necessary to make the throw. No one thinks about weight shift or how fast to move the arm forward to get the ball to the tree, or when to release the ball during the throwing motion. Students, no matter how athletic, pick up the ball and throw it at the tree. Some hit it, some don't, but all make the motion quickly and without any cerebral analysis.

The same is true of writing your name. If I ask you to sign your name, you can do it while carrying on a conversation. You can even sign your name with your eyes closed. It's easy: give it a try. Pick up a pen, find some paper, close your eyes, and sign your name.

Now, with your eyes open, I want you to try to copy your own signature exactly, concentrating on the motion of the pen and moving as slowly and carefully as possible.

Unless you are an artist or a skilled surgeon with abnormal tweezer dexterity, you won't come close to copying your original signature. And yet, if you closed your eyes again and signed the paper a second time, you would find that the sightless signature looks a lot closer to the original than the one you took painstaking care to try to perfect.

Whether it is signing your name, throwing a baseball, or hitting a golf shot, the less time you spend thinking about how to perform the skill, the more likely you are to achieve your desired result.

All great athletes apply this principle. Yankee shortstop Derek Jeter doesn't think as he scoops up a hard-hit grounder and throws it to first base. He doesn't have time to think. Derek feels the motion, reacts to a ball coming at him, makes the grab, looks at the first baseman, and throws. He hasn't had to think while making that move since he was in Little League.

Does anyone believe Peyton Manning thinks about how far to cock his arm or how fast to move his hand forward when he sees Marvin Harrison break free in the end zone? Does Jeff Gordon think about how much pressure to apply to the throttle of the 24 car when he's making a pass? Of course not: Manning, Jeter, Gordon, and all other noteworthy athletes react in split seconds. They don't think about the mechanics of what they're doing, because they don't have time.

Unfortunately, golfers have plenty of time for the mind to corrupt the process. The golf ball is stationary, and the game, for the most part, is static. No 300-pound tackles are rushing you in golf; nobody is throwing balls at you while you line up putts; and you aren't dodging cars traveling at 200 miles an hour. In a four-hour round, the average golfer spends about three minutes actually hitting shots. The rest of the time is spent traversing the course, talking to playing partners, figuring out what club to hit, waiting for the group ahead to move along, and going through all manner of preshot machinations, including practice swings, wiggles, waggles, hitches, twitches, and grunts. That's one of the main reasons golf broadcasts have never done well on radio. Announcers would spend hours vamping: "Well, he's walking . . . still walking . . . now standing . . . his right index finger is approaching his nostril."

All that wasted time creates havoc with the game. Players have trouble finding their rhythm, and their minds wander, often into areas of needless paranoia. "What if I top this shot: God, that would be embarrassing! What if I screw up my score by slipping back into my same old bad habits: that would be terrible. Now make sure you get the club inside on the takeaway."

The physically demanding parts aside, speed golf is actually much easier than traditional/slow golf, because so many of the distractions and obstacles are eliminated due to the nature of the game. There's no time to think; it's look, hit, and run.

Ironically, the fact that you have so much time to think makes golf tougher than if the ball were being thrown at you. Reacting to motion is a trait that has evolved in animals for thousands of years. Stand still when a bear is charging at you, and the bear will hesitate, confused by the fact that you aren't fleeing. In some cases the animal will lose interest in you and move on to other, more interesting prey.

Humans are more evolved than bears, but the same instincts apply. When a baseball is fouled off into the stands, nobody has to tell the fans sitting behind first base to raise their hands and duck their heads. When a valuable vase is falling off a table, you don't have to think about what to do. You reach out and grab the vase instinctively before it hits the floor.

But like the man who stands perfectly still in the face of an oncoming bear, the golf ball sits motionless, waiting on the golfer to do something to move it. This stillness confuses our basic instincts and allows our minds to fill with unwanted process thoughts.

A golfer might be able to get away with one swing thought during a round. "Slow takeaway" or "make a full turn" will sometimes work. Two swing thoughts create mental clutter. Three thoughts and things become jumbled. Four and you're looking at a slow, frustrating round. Unfortunately, most average golfers have dozens of thoughts plaguing their minds. Some struggling players even have 99 swing thoughts, but, alas, and with all apologies to Jay-Z, hitting the ball ain't one.

IS IT REALLY THAT EASY?

Will playing faster and thinking less really transform you from someone who struggles to break a hundred into a club champion or future Tour player? Of course not. No matter what speed you play, golf is hard (although not as hard as some people make it), and the only way to improve as a player is to spend the appropriate time developing the motor skills needed to hit the golf ball, and then put in hours of time on the course learning to get the ball in the hole in as few strokes as possible. Golfers often get frustrated in the learning process when they believe that if they understand intellectually and conceptually what is to be done, they will immediately be able to do it. Knowledge and information are not the most important elements in learning a new skill.

As my colleague Rick Martino, Director of Instruction for the PGA of America, recently quipped to me, "If information and knowledge were the most important aspects to good ball striking and playing golf, I'd be one of the best in the world." And although Rick is no slouch as a player, he's not on TV Sunday afternoons.

But the learning process doesn't have to be drudgery. Humans best learn motor skills through experience: trial and error and the related feedback. Good coaching can speed up the process, but none of us learned how to stand (a very early and basic motor skill) with verbal instruction: "Hey, Junior, lean more to the left and put your right arm out." At that age you didn't understand language, and even if you did, you didn't know where your weight should be centered. No matter what your parents said, you were going to fall down. You learned to stand by doing it, just like you hit a golf ball out of bounds at times and learned not to do it by teeing up another ball and trying it again.

A big part of trial-and-error learning is failure, such as the toddler falling down while trying to stand. Without failure, learning cannot take place. I'd like to replace or eliminate the word *failure* because of its terribly negative and misconstrued connotation. "Failure"—not performing the targeted task or attaining the desired outcome—provides phenomenal feedback. When you top a shot, hit one really crooked, or miss a short putt, it is considered "failing." Is that what you tell a kid who is trying to learn to ride a bike and falls off (which will happen)? That "failure" actually provides valuable feedback so that the mind-body system can learn the skill. So the next time you hit a squirrelly shot, rather than immediately saying "my bad," observe the outcome, get a feel for what happened, and get back on your golf bike and try again.

By learning through feel—focusing on the "what" rather than the "how-to"—and by working with what the body does naturally when you're trying to advance an object like a golf ball, you can make substantial strides in a relatively short time. And the swing thoughts that have been rattling around in your mind can be discarded like an old divot. Golf can be a reaction sport: a game where you forget about the mechanics and focus on getting the ball from point A to point B in as few strokes as possible.

The following pages show you how to transition from the "process" learner who thinks about the length of your backswing, the position of your hands at the top, your weight shift, and your swing plane, to a "feel" learner who builds his own individual set of fundamentals by focusing on the tasks at hand. In time, you will be able to forget about the mechanics of your swing and think about nothing but getting the golf ball into the hole. I will show you what to practice and how to practice, but I will also show you how to lower your scores by relaxing and getting out of your own way.

Some of the concepts presented will simply seem too good to be true. Do not forget that the foremost learners in the world—the Tiger Woodses of learning—are children, specifically from the time they are born up until about three years of age. The vastness and complexity of what is learned during those years, both motor functions and other, is unparalleled. And this great learning is all done unconsciously. The information I present and the suggestions I make are based on research and neuroscience from experts in the motor-learning field and from my own personal experience. The goal is to have you build and learn these vital skills in as little time as possible and in the way that is best suited to you.

In the process, I'll help you identify the 99 swing thoughts thumping around in your head and show you how to transform those thoughts into "games" and "tasks" that will allow your body to learn instinctively. I prefer those words to "drills" (sounds like you are going to the dentist) and "exercises" (sounds like you might be some nutball running around the golf course). Besides, ask kids to do a drill or exercise and you've probably lost them; ask them to play a game—or just tell them *what* to do instead of *how to* do it—and you've aroused curiosity, interest, and imagination. Kids play games for the fun of it. Isn't that why you started to play golf in the first place? In playing, kids learn. Better to "play to learn" than to "learn to play."

Most important, I'll teach you how to put John Daly's point-and-shoot theory into practice. I will show you how to become a look–swing, aim–fire, freewheeling, react-to-the-target golfer who feels the game, plays faster, shoots lower scores, and has more fun.

In the process (and in deference to Dr. Suzuki), I use music references, like the title of the book. These are designed as not-so-subtle reminders of all those songs you haven't thought about in years but can still sing in the shower without missing a lyric. Once you learn to use that part of your brain on the golf course, you will be able to clear your mind of those 99 brain-freezing swing thoughts and get on with the business of getting the ball in the hole.

"WHO NEEDS YA, BABY?"

Rushing off to get my speed-golf gear organized one evening after a long day on the lesson tee, I hastily put my clubs in the specially designed speed-golf bag and headed to the first tee.

As I arrived at the first green, I realized I'd forgotten something—my putter. I considered running back to get it, but instead decided that, for the rest of the round, I would simply putt with whichever club I had used to hit onto the green. What the heck, I normally play speed golf with only six clubs, what's one less? . . .

The bottom line with putting is, you are basically rolling a ball to a hole with an object. Could be a putter, could be a wedge—could be your shoe. So I played the front nine at Ghost Creek putting with my gap wedge, 8-iron, 5-iron, and 4-metal. I three-putted once and had a couple of kick-ins with the wedge after nice short shots from around the green.

As I headed over to the tenth tee, dusk began to settle in. I figured I'd play a few more holes and call it a night. That's when the putterless birdie barrage began. I made an easy 4 on the par-five tenth by belly rolling (striking the middle or equator of the ball with the leading edge of the club) my gap wedge into the hole after a nice approach shot. On eleven, a 175-yardish par-three, I cut a little 5-iron in to about fifteen feet and rolled in the downhill left-to-righter, with, of course, the 5-iron. I hit it about twenty feet on the par-four twelfth with the 8-iron and rolled that one in as well. I stuck an 8-iron six feet on the par-four thirteenth and calmly rolled the putt in, again with the 8-iron.

By the time I got to the downhill, 220-yard, par-three fourteenth hole, it was beginning to get dark. I decided to make this my last hole, as the green was in proximity to the clubhouse. I conveniently hit my 4-metal about fifteen feet above the hole—and rolled that "putt" in for my fifth consecutive birdie, this time using the 4-metal to roll my rock.

As I walked (it was time for a break) off the fourteenth green, it hit me what I'd just done: I'd just birdied five holes in a row while running—without a putter. I've never birdied those holes consecutively before or since that moment, and I've played them dozens of times with my trusty flatstick in the bag and plenty of time to read the green.

Later that evening, I began to contemplate what had happened and why. What had I been "thinking about" over those putts? Did I have a particular putting/swing thought? The answer was in fact that I had taken myself back to a "kid stage," where all I was focused on was playing the game and the task at hand: rolling the ball into the hole with whatever implement was in my hands. The mind-body system is remarkable when we stay out of its way and the conscious mind stops trying to tell it how to do things.

Not once did I think about having my eyes over the ball, making a pendulum-like stroke, or keeping my head still. I had a ball, a variety of different clubs, and in looking at the line and seeing what I wanted to do, I was extremely successful.

Lesson to be learned: next time you are really struggling with your putting and you feel as if your mind is cluttered with such an abundance of mechanical and technical info on how to putt, go out to the putting green with a wedge, an iron, or even a driver, and begin to putt. You will have to throw all your shoulder-rocking and putter-head-arching thoughts away, because suddenly they are no longer relevant. You will look at the ball, the line, and the hole and simply try to figure out, instinctively, how to get the ball rolling on the line at the right speed with whatever you are putting with. That's exactly where your focus needs to be at all times—exactly what a child focuses on if you give him a club and a ball and tell him to roll the ball into the hole. They don't want to be told how to do it. Give them a task/game and leave them alone to figure out what works best for them.

ONE

○ ○ ○

"Papa Was a Rollin' Stone"

But Could He Putt?

"Rolling the stone (rock)," or as the less hip among us call it, "putting," is arguably the most important part of the game, and the putter is the most crucial scoring club in your bag. If you don't believe me, count the number of shots you hit with each club during your last round. Go ahead. I'll wait.

Depending on what you shot and the difficulty of your golf course, you probably hit your driver ten to fourteen times. If you're a fairway wood sort of person, you might have hit your 3-, 4-, 5-, or 7-wood a couple of times each. Then you probably hit 6- or 7-irons once or twice each, a few more with your wedges. You most likely left a couple of clubs in your bag, never swinging them a single time. But, if you honestly counted your shots, about thirty or more of the strokes you took in your last round were struck with the putter. If you had a phenomenal putting day, the number might have been twenty-five or twenty-six. If you gacked a few, you could have had thirty-six, thirty-seven, or even forty putts, far and away the most strokes taken with any club in your bag. Granted, a few of those putts may have been kick-ins, but nonetheless, the short club with the least amount of loft gets a huge amount of use.

This should be good news. The putting stroke is the smallest motion in golf, the shot with the fewest moving parts that requires the least amount of physical exertion. All you have to do is roll the ball from point A to point B. No long, full shoulder turns; no delayed releases, full extensions, or weight shifts: you just roll the ball into the hole. What could be easier?

Unfortunately, golfers tend to complicate even the simplest of motions. If you hand a child a putter and tell him to roll the ball in the hole in the fewest number of strokes, he will, with a little practice, become a pretty good putter. But if you tell the child to

- hold the putter with an inverse overlap grip,

- stand with his feet shoulder-width apart so that an imaginary vector bisecting both his big toes will run parallel to the intended path of his putt,

- flex his knees,

- bow at the hips, keeping his spine angle straight,

- position the ball so that his dominant eye is "behind" the ball,

- use a pendulum stroke initiated between the shoulder blades,

- keep the hands, wrists, knees, and head "quiet,"

- accelerate the clubhead through the ball while maintaining the angle of the left wrist throughout the stroke,

- and don't look up until the ball is five feet away,

you might as well ask the poor kid to create a cold fusion reactor. If he tries half of those things, he'll be so tied up in knots he will be lucky to make contact. And these aren't all the putting thoughts that are taught, not by a long shot.

Said 2006 U.S. Open champion Geoff Ogilvy about Sergio García's recent putting woes, "It looks to me like there is too much 'thinking' and not enough 'doing' going on."

But if you give the kid an iPod with some rhythmic music, hand him ten balls, and tell him to roll as many as he can into the hole from fifteen feet away, he'll make three or four while he sings the chorus of the latest Pussycat Dolls tune. Give him an hour and no instruction and he'll make 50 percent of the putts from fifteen feet. In addition to the rhythmic benefits, the music is occupying the kid's conscious mind, the part that likes to tell us how to do things.

Putting fits our music analogy better than any other part of the game, because good putting, like good singing, is 1 percent mechanics and 99 percent feel. To sing well you have to be able to hear the notes you are trying to hit, open your mouth and your throat, breathe with your diaphragm, and enunciate the lyrics while modulating your pitch by tightening and loosening the vocal cords. And if you think about any of that during a good tune, you'll howl like one of those *American Idol* contestants Simon Cowell calls "dreadful."

Good putters don't think about the mechanics of their strokes while they are on the golf course. There are a bazillion different ways to putt well, and everyone's way is going to be different. As putting guru Jackie Burke Jr. said, "The best way to putt is the way you putt best."

The one thing all great putters have in common is that they look at the hole, visualize the break and the speed the ball needs to travel to get there, and hit it. Any thoughts about the stroke will interfere with your ability to make the putt. The technical or mechanical aspects relevant to good putting, whether that be in the preputt routine or something in the stroke itself, have all been learned, through rehearsal and correct repetition, *prior to* pulling the trigger.

Wynton Marsalis doesn't think about the fingering of his trumpet in the middle of a concert. He feels the music and moves his fingers out of instinct, like punching the remote controls on a video game. The mechanics of putting are a lot simpler than the fingering of a jazz trumpet, so learning to putt through feel and instinct makes a lot more sense than thinking about the litany of mechanics in your stroke.

Besides, every individual's technique and mechanics will vary, depending on what works best for them. On a putting green, Bobby Locke didn't look much like George Archer, and José María Olazábal and Ben Crenshaw's styles and strokes do not vaguely resemble one another. Yet their techniques all work brilliantly— for them.

"THE WINDMILL SONG"

The Johnson Brothers' 1971 hit mentioned in the above head had absolutely nothing to do with putting, but the title offers a chance to make an important point. If you've ever played Putt-Putt, you know the concept of the windmill hole. The arms of the windmill cover the hole as they rotate, which means you not only have to putt the ball on a line and speed to make it through the hole, you also have to time your stroke so that the ball gets there while the hole is unobstructed. If your timing is off, the windmill knocks your ball into Captain Hook's Puddle Pond.

And yet the most inexperienced putters—kids as young as five who have never held a club in their lives—can putt a golf ball through the windmill. This miracle of biomechanics is possible because the Putt-Putt golfer doesn't think about the mechanics of her stroke. She focuses solely on timing her shot to avoid the arms of the windmill. In so doing, she uses the same part of the brain that tells you when to raise your hand and close your fingers to catch a ball that has been thrown at you. You don't think about which muscles you use, or the angle of your wrist when you catch the ball. You look at the oncoming object and react. At the windmill hole, you look at the pace of the windmill and time your stroke accordingly.

In speed golf, there are no windmills, but I have very little time to contemplate much of anything. In the middle of a forty-five-minute round of golf, I barely have time to catch my breath, let alone verify that my shoulders are square or that my putter face is perpendicular to the putting line at impact. So I've got to trust my fundamentals and mechanics and react to the putting picture in front of me. Actually, not having much time is often a blessing in disguise, for it doesn't allow my all-knowing and ever-interfering conscious side to convolute the motion.

Research in neuroscience now tells us that part of the difficulty in putting is that it is too easy. You have a stable, static stance and a lot of time to prepare for the task; you have a stationary target and have executed exactly the same movement thousands of times. The reason kids putt well at the windmill hole is that, from a purely neurological standpoint, the brain organizes things better when the target is moving.

Unfortunately, in real golf you don't have a windmill. If you did, you would have to use the portion of your brain that deals with timing and rhythm. Too often, I see students working on the mechanics of their strokes while they're trying to make a twenty-footer for par. As a result, these students stare at the ball for an interminable number of seconds, forgetting all about the hole and the path of ground the ball needs to traverse in order to go in. If they do look at the hole, it's only for a second and only because that's one of the items on their mental checklist. This is like staring at the dart instead of the dartboard—not a good idea, especially in a crowded bar.

To make more putts, every player must forget about his stroke and focus on the line and hole, just as you would have to if the windmill is covering it. In fact, if need be, *look at the hole instead of the ball*. After all, the hole is the ultimate destination and, last I checked, the greatest free-throw shooters in NBA history were all looking at the basket, not the ball.

The best way to develop your putting stroke is to practice with a purpose; that is, you have to have a specific idea of what you're trying to accomplish and have accurate feedback. There is no magic bullet in putting, but I see far too many players practicing their putting without a clear idea of just what it is they need to do. They hit putt after putt without any real purpose or goal, which, in my opinion, is a monumental waste of time.

To make the process more effective, and more fun, I believe you have to play games with yourself on the putting green. These putting games are divided into two categories, much as they need to be for other parts of the game:

1. Games that help you develop and learn the motor skill

2. Tasks that help simulate a playing situation

Some good ones to get you started follow.

(ROLL THE) "ROCK AROUND THE CLOCK"

Every day, from the moment he first picked up a horn until the day he died as one of the greatest musicians of all time, Miles Davis went through one of the most elementary of musical drills: he practiced his scales. In the beginning, running through the scales was no easy feat. Like all early-learning musicians, Miles had to get the fingering and lip positions down. But even after he became accomplished, he continued to practice the scales, simply because they are the most fundamental element in music, and even the greats can never lose touch with the fundamentals.

To translate that same philosophy to the putting green, find a five- to ten-foot putt that has a fair amount of break from all sides. Mark off five "stations" with tees, each station with a different break and slope (uphill, downhill, right to left, left to right). Begin at any station, and for four minutes, hit putts that enter the hole in a different way. Create a mental picture of how you want the ball to go in the hole, and putt.

For example, say to yourself: "I want this putt to die in the right edge of the hole." You can create a multitude of pictures by changing speeds and envisioning precisely where and how you want the ball to go in: firm, medium, and die in the hole—left edge, left center, dead center, right center, and right edge.

You get three tries at each mental picture. If unsuccessful, you have to change how you want the ball to go in at that station. If you can't hit it hard in the back center of the hole on a downhill left-to-right putt, change the mental picture and die it in the left edge of the hole instead.

As soon as you have made a putt with the chosen image, change pictures. Then repeat the same scenario at each station. This drill provides twenty minutes (most people's maximum concentration time) of intense, highly beneficial training.

When you walk away, you will have a greater understanding of how to read greens and how to visualize putts going in. Good green reading starts with a specific "mini motion picture" of how we want the ball to go in the hole. Just categorizing a putt as "uphill and left to right" isn't enough. It would be like telling a top dart player to just hit the board. You may find a specific way or speed that fits your putting best, and your green reading can then blossom with that preference.

"IT'S SO EASY"

During one of my first sessions as a student of the legendary Paul Runyan, who was known in golf circles as "Little Poison" for his Lilliputian stature and killer instinct, Paul had me practice a putting drill that left me shaking my head.

"I want you to put several balls in a circle no more than a foot from the hole, and make every one of them," he said.

As silly as I thought the drill was, I did as I was told. After making fifteen in a row from one foot (heck, I couldn't miss from that distance), I mustered up enough courage to ask Paul why he wanted me practicing putts I was never going to miss.

Paul gave a very serious stare before saying, "Do you have any idea how good it is for your mind, for your confidence, and for your psyche to see and hear the ball go in the hole every time?"

I didn't at the time, but as I have continued to practice the one-foot drill I have become a better putter.

You will, too.

Christopher building confidence by making one-foot putts.

Take three balls and place them in different spots around the hole, each one about a foot away. Go through your preshot routine, just as you would if you were playing. Get used to seeing, hearing, and feeling the ball go into the hole. This simple task will boost your confidence the next time you have a putt of any length that matters during a round. Imagine that—never missing.

Consistently making one-footers is the first step in achieving unconscious competency on the putting green. Plus, it will teach you to aim better and start your putts on line. And it is a task you should continue to practice forever, no matter how proficient you become. Just as Miles Davis practiced his scales until he died, you should spend a few minutes making one-footers on the clock during every practice session. It is an amazing way to tune your mind in to making more putts.

"BEAUTIFUL DISTRACTION"

Unless you know absolutely nothing about the game or have been living in a cave for the past decade, you probably know the story of Earl Woods honing Tiger's focus by trying to distract him. Earl would cough, jingle change, shout, or drop a club in the middle of Tiger's backswing, anything to break his concentration. After a while, Tiger became immune to the distractions. He didn't even hear Earl, and when he did, he didn't let the noise take him out of his routine.

To become a good putter, I think you need a mental distraction, something that will loosen you up, clear your mind, and allow you to make a relaxed stroke.

Have you ever noticed how much better you putt when you've already conceded that three-footer to yourself? You seem to be able to make any putt that doesn't matter, because you're relaxed and couldn't care less if the ball goes in or not. You're just stroking it for practice, or to get it out of the way. But when you have to make that three-footer to win the match, or when you need to two-putt to shoot your lowest score ever, the putter suddenly feels like a foreign object, and the hole shrinks to the size of a thimble.

Did you suddenly forget how to putt when the pressure was on? Did you lose all coordination and touch, the second the game was on the line? No, but you did experience a change. The same brain chemicals that allowed cavemen to flee from saber-toothed tigers cause your heart rate to jump, your breathing to quicken, and your muscles to tense when you feel pressure on the golf course.

Of course, it's easy to say to yourself, "Relax, take it easy. It's just golf. This is not life or death. If I make this putt, great; if I don't, my kids will still love me." But that doesn't always work. In fact, when given the choice of holding a venomous snake or having to make a three-footer in front of a gallery, most people say, "Hand over the viper."

It's not your fault. Chemicals like adrenaline, serotonin, dopamine, and endorphins have developed over millions of years of evolution. In the right circumstances, they can save your life. Unfortunately, you can't will yourself into turning off that spigot. These chemicals can't distinguish between the pressure of a four-foot putt and the anxiety you feel when being chased by a wild animal.

You can, however, trick your brain into minimizing the effects of these game-killers. And the best way to trick yourself is by practicing the art of distraction and by accepting reality.

Before he strokes a short putt, no matter how important, Brad Faxon, long considered one of the best putters on tour, convinces himself that he has just made a thousand putts in a row, and this one, the thousand and first, doesn't mean anything. By not caring whether or not the ball goes in and convincing himself he has already completed the task a thousand times, Fax makes more than his share of putts.

If there were such a thing as a "care meter," a device that measured just how much we care or how hard we are trying on a scale from one (don't give a rat's ass) to ten (grinding and trying as hard as humanly possible), we would all perform our best at around a six or a seven. Trying harder does not always produce better results. Give trying *less* a shot. You'll be surprised by the results.

Other players have played similar tricks with their minds. Ben Crane, also one of the best putters on tour, pretends to be Ben Crenshaw when he's over a putt. He even goes so far as imagining that he can see Crenshaw, who is regarded as one of the greatest putters in history, standing in his stead, while he, Crane, watches from the sideline.

These tricks of the brain take practice, but they are effective. There are other things you can do to create positive distractions as well.

You also need to accept the fact that golf is not life-or-death. Evel Knievel laughs when he hears about the pressure and fear involved with golf and what Tour players are going through every week. You miss a three-footer: big deal! The earth is not going to open up and swallow you, nor will you be forced to walk through a minefield. It's a game. Besides, if you made every three-footer, at some point you'd quit because it would be too easy.

Evel's game of choice was a bit riskier. If he failed on one of his jumps, the result was quite possibly death, not embarrassment or loss of a few dollars. "Tour players don't even play for their own money!" Evel reminds us. When you're staring at the Snake River Canyon, shallow breathing and sweaty palms are excusable. Standing over a putt that means nothing to your life or the lives of others is no biggie.

So cool your jets on the caring scale, and enjoy the challenge and fun of the game. Your performance will improve once you accept that making or missing a putt does not alter humanity.

"LISTEN TO THE MUSIC"

In the age of iPods and other MP3 players, it's not uncommon to see half the people on the putting green wearing headphones and listening to music. This is a perfect distraction, a great form of self-hypnosis, and an efficient way to quiet the incessant chatter of the conscious mind.

Find a song you love that also has a beat that matches your natural rhythm. If you have a slow pace in your walk, talk, and swing, you don't want to choose something from Twisted Sister. Pick a song that matches the tempo of your life. If you can walk, talk, and swing a club to the beat of a song, it's probably right. In my case it's "Let It Grow" by Eric Clapton or almost anything by Sheryl Crow.

Another option to clear the mind and improve tempo is to use a metronome. Set it somewhere about fifty-seven to sixty-five beats per minute, again depending on your natural rhythm and pace. Start the putter away on a chosen "beep" and hit the putt on the very next one. Tick-tock, one-two. Focusing on catching and matching the tones will help rid you of putting stroke thoughts, and the tempo established can be carried to other clubs and shots.

Now put the song you've chosen on your MP3 player and set it on endless repeat, just like when you were a kid playing the same new record

Christopher putting with an iPod.

over and over. With the song playing in your ears, practice two-, three-, and four-footers until you are confident you can make most, if not all, of them. And as much as you might want to, don't change the song.

This might not sound like much of a task, but after a while, the brain will automatically equate three-footers with your chosen song. Then, the next time you have a pressure-packed putt to close out a match, just sing your song to yourself, and your mind will go back to the putting green. By focusing on the music, you will distract your conscious mind so you can relax and make the putt.

"I'VE GOT SPEED"

Despite all the gobbledygook you've heard and read about putting, only two things matter when it comes to making putts. You have to roll the ball at a speed that will get it in the hole and hit it on the right line for the speed you've chosen. Get those two things right, and the ball's going in, no matter how you've gripped the putter, where your feet are pointing, or which hand is more dominant in your stroke. Line and speed are the only variables that count on the green.

And each of those variables is dependent on the other. For example, if you have a ten-foot putt that breaks left to right, the amount of break in the putt is totally dependent on how hard you hit it. If you ram the ball in the back of the hole, the putt might only break a couple of inches. If you let it die in the left side, the putt might break a foot.

Just as there are many ways to play a hundred-yard shot into a green, there are a number of ways to make every putt. In most cases, there is a trough several inches wide in which a putt can be made. The variable is speed. The harder you strike the putt, the less it will break. The softer you hit it, the more effect the slope of the green will have on the ball.

Of the two variables in putting, speed is the most important. The reason is simple: if you misread the break of a putt by a foot (a big misread) but hit the ball the correct speed, you will have left yourself a one-foot tap-in. But if you read the break correctly and miss the speed, you might run the ball ten feet past the hole or leave it five feet short.

So how do you learn to roll putts the correct speed, especially when the texture of the greens varies from day to day, or even from hour to hour, depending on the conditions? You certainly can't learn analytically. Trying to calculate how far to take the putter head back and how fast to accelerate through the putt is like trying to vary the distance between the letters in your name as you sign a check.

One of the best games for learning to control your speed is to putt to the fringe instead of the hole. Place five balls at various

Christopher putting balls to the fringe with eyes closed, then checking to verify "feel."

spots on the green between five and twenty-five feet from the fringe. Now putt each ball as close as you can to the fringe without any of the balls rolling off the green. After each putt, close your eyes so you can't see where it ended up. Before looking up to check, ask yourself where you think the ball finished. Then take a peek. This process is extremely important in developing feel for distance. Your guesses will improve with practice, and soon you will have a pretty good idea where your balls stopped without even looking.

Repeat this game from various distances, and from different spots so that you are putting uphill, downhill, and across the hill. Don't stop until you can roll every ball to within a few inches of the fringe without going off the putting surface.

"WALK THE LINE"

The other variable in making putts is picking the right line and hitting the ball on the line that you've picked. Most golfers don't pick the line correctly, however, and even when they do, they don't hit the ball anywhere close to the line they've chosen.

One of the things I do in my putting clinics is ask students to line up a fifteen-foot putt that breaks nine inches. Before anyone hits the putt, each student has to guess how much it breaks. The guesses range from six inches to "that putt is straight." No one guesses that the putt breaks nine inches. Almost everyone under-reads it. The same thing happens when I move to a twenty-five-footer that breaks three feet. My students guess that the putt breaks eighteen, maybe twenty, inches. Rarely does someone read three feet of break. Short-game instructor and putting researcher extraordinaire Dave Pelz has found that most people underread putts by about 50 percent—then hit them 50 percent too hard to compensate for the misread.

After a great deal of study, I've determined that this is because golfers don't analyze the terrain between their ball and the hole. They look at a small area around the ball and the small area around the hole. And although the five feet or so on the putting line in front of the hole is important because that is where the ball will be traveling at its slowest and be most influenced by the slope, the twenty or so feet of turf in between is not vapor.

This underreading happens even though most golfers take several minutes reading their putts, much longer than they need to figure out the proper break. Studies have shown that humans take in close to eleven million bits of information per second, ten million of which are taken in visually. Scientists have calculated this number by counting the number of receptor cells in each sense organ and the nerves that go from these cells to the brain. With all that information coming in, why do you need five minutes to read a putt?

In speed golf, I'm always asked if I line up putts. The answer is: "Sure, I line up every putt. I just do it as I'm running up to the green and in the few seconds I have on the green prior to putting." Judging the contour of the ground you're on is not much different from judging the direction and intensity of the wind. In five seconds, my system (and yours) has taken in approximately fifty million bits of information. What more do I need?

If you were blindfolded, it wouldn't take long for you to figure out if you were walking uphill, downhill, or along the side of a hill. Your inner ear tells you the slope of the terrain. When I'm running up to a green, I can, within a couple of seconds, determine where the high and low points are on the putting surface. Plus, greens are designed so that water has to drain somewhere. Ninety percent of them slope from back to front. Knowing that fact ahead of time helps. Once I have the big-picture topography figured out, the subtleties are a lot easier to see when I'm standing over my putt.

"HIT THAT MONEY MAKER"

Christopher putting a ball over a quarter.

For this game, I want you to simply roll the ball over a quarter, starting at eighteen inches away and then progressively moving to three feet, and then six. Focus on a small target, trying to get the ball rolling over the center of the quarter each time. If you miss, pull the ball back and try again. Avoid thinking about why you missed. Just continue to roll the ball over the quarter.

Like the infant learning to stand upright, starting the ball online is something that is learned through the trial-and-error feedback you get from failure. When the child falls, it may hurt, but the tumble provides critical kinesthetic and proprioceptic information. If your ball rolls over a side of the quarter or misses it completely, you have not failed; you have provided yourself with an opportunity to learn. Use that feedback and adjust accordingly.

All great putters learn through trial and error and perhaps a little coaching. But each has his or her own individual way of starting the ball on line.

Once you have found the best setup and putting stroke for you, make a note of it. Either with the use of a mirror, other training aid, or a video camera, take note of your posture, exact distance from the ball, eye and ball position, and so on. Seeing yourself in your ideal position, making the stroke that best works for you, is extremely useful in learning and ingraining the habit. I strongly advise you to keep a visual record of your success so that you may refer back to it at a future date.

Once you've improved your ability to start the ball on line and roll the ball at the right speed, you'll have a better idea of how good your green reading is. The following game will help you with both.

"JUST BETWEEN YOU AND ME"

Christopher putting a ball through two tees.

Place two tees about a foot or so in front of your ball on the putting line, spaced apart just enough so that the ball can go through them, like goalposts. Choose a putt of five to twenty-five feet that has some break. You will want to read the putt first so you can picture the path the ball must travel.

After hitting the putt, you will have some very important points of feedback:

1. If your ball hits one of the tees, you did not start your ball on the intended line—time to go back to the "rolling the ball over the quarter" game.

2. If the ball goes between the tees but doesn't go in the hole, you have successfully started the ball on your intended line, but you have misread the putt. From here, you can either try the putt on the same lie at a different speed or move the tees.

"I GOTTA MOVE FASTER"

With a partner, find two holes about fifteen feet apart and place three balls next to each hole. You start at one hole, your partner at the other. The first person to make ten putts wins. Once you've hit your three, *run or walk quickly* to the hole, and putt them back. You are trying to make as many as possible, since the winner is the first to ten. But you will also learn that the more attempts you get, the better your chances of getting to ten before your opponent. You will start to putt in the most effective and natural way—simply looking and doing.

You'll also find yourself chatting and chiding your opponent as the game goes on. You'll be in constant motion, looking and reacting, having fun (a critical aspect of learning) without time for swing thoughts. Hmm, sounds like putting during a round of speed golf. . . .

WHAT YOU CAN LEARN FROM SPEED GOLF

In speed golf I am running between shots at a clip that many people would consider a dead sprint. The game is golf's equivalent of circuit training. It's an Olympic biathlon on grass instead of snow, with a funny-looking stick instead of a rifle. I run, stop, hit a shot, and take off again. Because I repeat this process over an eighteen-hole golf course (covering between four and six miles), I have to work hard to control my breathing and keep my heart rate out of aerobic range.

Believe it or not, running to the greens actually helps my putting. My heart rate is going down after I stop running and stand over my putt. My hands are also relaxed, since most of my energy is being spent getting my heart, lungs, and legs into recovery. These are the physical elements you need to putt well. I just happen to get them by sprinting from the fairway to the green.

While you might not want to run away from your playing partners, picking up the pace, focusing on your breathing, effectively using your visual system, and making sure your hands and arms are loose enough to run a hundred-yard dash at any moment will do wonders for your putting.

○ ○ ○

"Lay Your Hands on Me"

Just as every hit song starts with fundamentals—a consistent rhythm, a memorable melody, and an easy bridge—every good golf shot begins with the basics. The three basics you will find in every well-played shot are consistent grip, setup, and alignment. That is not to say that all great golfers grip the club the same way; they don't. Nor do they all set up to the ball and align themselves to the target the same. Great songwriters don't all compose music the same way, and great golfers don't prepare to hit golf shots in a uniform fashion. What both musicians and champion golfers do, however, is master the fundamentals that work for them and repeat those fundamentals consistently.

Mozart sat at a table with a quill in his hand and wrote every part to entire symphonies. Paul McCartney pecked out new songs with two fingers on a piano. Both did pretty well at their craft. Along those same lines, Ben Hogan gripped a golf club with his left thumb pointing straight down the shaft so that when he looked down, he could see only one knuckle, that of the left index finger. David Duval became the number-one player in the world with his left hand turned so far to the right (strong) he could see every knuckle on its back. Both those players got the job done with completely different grips, but ones that worked for them.

Ed Fiori played well for years with a grip teachers used to refer to as a "Harley-Davidson," one with the right hand turned so far under the club that it looked like Ed was about to rev the engine of a motorcycle. Fred Couples and Paul Azinger ride their hogs in the same posse as Ed with their superstrong hand positions. Jack Nicklaus won most of his majors with what we call a "neutral" grip, where the palms faced each other, but as equipment changed and he got a little older, Jack strengthened his grip to keep up with change. The grips on Nicklaus's clubs were, themselves, slick and worn, a reminder to hold the club lightly. Tiger Woods won three U.S. Amateur titles with his left hand on top of the club and right hand turned slightly under, but as he got stronger and began retooling his game, the grip became more neutral.

Claude Harmon, winner of the 1948 Masters and one of the greatest teachers of all time, wrapped his left thumb around the club as if it were a baseball bat, while Albert Crews makes a good living playing senior golf gripping the club cross-handed.

And let's not forget Billy Burke, winner of the 1931 U.S. Open (it took a record seventy-two-hole playoff with George Von Elm to decide this one). Burke became the first player to win a major championship with steel-shafted clubs—and he did it with fewer than ten fingers, as he was missing the pinkie on his left hand.

The moral of the story is: there are as many ways to grip the club as there are different ways to write music. But just as the songwriter's goal is to produce a hit, the golfer's goal is to develop a grip that will produce consistent golf shots.

"WHY ARE YOU HOLDING ME SO CLOSE?"

The preceding lyrics come from *The King and I,* which means I'm willing to dig deep to prove a point. The point is, you can't learn the perfect golf grip by reading a book, just as there aren't any how-to manuals for writing the next hit song. A good golf grip is whatever grip works best for you. To understand that, you have to understand what you are hoping to accomplish when you grip the club, and why the grip is so important.

In the six hundred years that people have been playing golf, the first fundamental has always been the laying of hands on the golf club. This makes sense, because the only contact the player has with the ball is through the club, and the only contact he or she has with the club is through the grip. The club hits the ball; your hands hold the club. Simple.

But that is just the backbeat of the opening bars. Things get more complicated from there.

If holding on to the club were the only goal of the grip, players would split their hands and hold the club like a farm tool. While you'll find a lot of different grips among the greatest players in the world, you won't see anybody holding a driver like a pickax. The reason is that the goal of the golf swing is to hit the ball to a target. To do that you have to control where the clubface points at impact, and what path the clubhead travels when it makes contact with the ball.

You might be a strong, coordinated athlete who can generate a 125-mph swing speed, but if your clubface is pointing fifty yards right of the target, you probably won't be able to find the ball. And if the clubface is pointing toward the target, but the club-head is swinging on a path thirty yards left, the ball will spin wildly to the right, the kind of slice golf magazines have been promising to cure for fifty years. Conversely, if you swing on a great path, but the clubface is pointing thirty yards left, the shot is going to be a low, smothering hook, the kind of shot Ben Hogan called "the terror of the field mice." A swing path that takes the club well right of the target will impart counterclock-wise spin on the ball and the shot will hook out of play.

A good grip is one that allows you to deliver the club to the ball with a square clubface (one pointing toward the target). Once the clubface is square, you have a chance to swing the clubhead on a path somewhere on the line you want the ball to go. Where the clubface is pointing will always dictate the path, not vice versa. Ask any chronic slicer if he has ever tried to swing the club on an "out-to-in" path, and he will undoubtedly respond no. Yet he does so consistently. Why? His mind and body have unconsciously learned to compensate for an open clubface, often the result of a poor grip to start with.

The best grip to achieve a square clubface at impact will vary depending on your strengths, weaknesses, and preferences. If you have weak hands but a strong lower body, you will grip the club differently than does someone with chicken legs who is always being handed the difficult-to-open mayonnaise jar because his hands are so strong. If you naturally generate a lot of clubhead speed at impact, your grip will be different from the grip of some- one who struggles to swing the driver sixty miles an hour.

Equipment also plays a big role in how you grip the club. Back in the hickory-shafted days, grips were much stronger than they are today, because the torque of the shafts required a lot more hand action to square the clubface at impact. As technology ad- vanced and shafts became lighter and stronger, good players could weaken their grips because they didn't have to manipulate the clubface at impact. This change didn't come about instantly. Nobody put out a press release that said, "Hey, guys, you can weaken your grip now; we got that shaft-torque thing worked out." There were no charts printed that said you could weaken your grip two degrees for every three-gram reduction in shaft weight, and nobody held teaching seminars where "Weaken the Grip for Today's Modern Equipment" was discussed.

The way golfers gripped the club evolved over time through trial and error. Hogan probably dug his grip "out of the dirt" (lots of practice) as well, realizing only after going broke twice that in order to stop hooking the ball, he needed to weaken—hands turned to the left on the handle—his grip. In so doing, he became one of the greatest ball strikers and players ever—and may have inadvertently started a generation of slicers for those who imitated him. The only goal that mattered was finding a way to generate maximum clubhead speed at the moment of impact and square the clubface so that it pointed where the player wanted the ball to go. Golfers experimented until they found the best way to grip the club to accomplish those goals.

There are no rules that say you must grip the club a certain way. You can hold it inverted, cross-handed, and double-jointed if you want; but if you do, you probably won't square the clubface with any consistency.

Fortunately, you don't have to learn the entire grip on your own. Just as four-four music has four beats per measure whether the song is by Dawn Upshaw or 50 Cent, good golf grips have a few fundamentals that are universal to all players regardless of skill level or physical condition.

"ALL I GOTTA DO IS ACT NATURALLY"

I'm not sure how much golf Buck Owens played in Bakersfield, but if the country crooner played at all, he could have heeded the advice of his most famous song lyrics when learning the grip.

The best golf grip for you is the one that accentuates what you do naturally. For example, if you stand with your arms hanging relaxed, most of you will notice that your left palm does not face your side (unless you naturally stand at attention). Your left hand (for right-handed golfers, the top hand on the handle of the club) hangs with the palm facing somewhere between your left side and directly behind you, usually a spot near or just behind your left buttock. This naturally hanging position is where your left hand will be when you grip the golf club.

To experiment with this, stand erect and relax your arms. In fact, shake the arms and hands to get the tension out as Michael Phelps would do before jumping into the pool to take a swim. Then, without changing the position of your arm or hand, bring the club to your side and grip it in your left hand. (If you put the club in front of your body your hand will turn counterclockwise, a "catching" reflex, resulting in a "weak" left-hand grip position.) Don't rotate your wrist, or otherwise manipulate your hand position; just grip the club the way your hand and arm naturally hang at your side.

Now look down at your left hand. Some of you will be able to see all four knuckles, because the natural position of your palm points more behind you than toward your side. Others of you will only be able to see a knuckle or two. You are the people whose

LEFT: Christopher standing with his arms hanging naturally at his side. RIGHT: Christopher in the same standing position holding a golf club in his left hand, focusing on how the hand's position has not changed from the previous picture.

hands hang more palms-facing. Neither of these grips is right or wrong. But the one that most closely mirrors how your left hand naturally hangs is the best grip for you. That's your "neutral" position.

The right-hand grip is a little different, but just as natural. To get the feel for where your right hand should be on the club, reach out to shake hands with someone. When you shake another person's hand, your wrist cocks slightly downward so that your fingers are pointing toward the person's shoes and the palm of your hand is facing directly to your left.

This is what your right hand will look like when it is on the golf club. To get a sense of that feeling, reach out to shake hands with an imaginary acquaintance, then put your right hand on a golf club without altering the position of your hand and arm. Some of you will have your palm facing directly to your left;

Christopher putting right hand on tip of shaft and sliding down over left thumb.

some will have the palm facing more toward the ground; and some will have it facing more upward. But wherever you naturally put your hand during a handshake is where it ought to fall when you're gripping a club.

In addition, the right-hand grip is primarily a "finger grip," with the handle of the club resting in the fingers and away from the palm of the hand. To capture this feel, hold the club vertically and place the right hand on the shaft at the very tip, near the clubhead. Instinctively, you will grasp the shaft in the fingers—not the palm—because the club is skinny at that point. Then slide the right hand down the shaft and cover the thumb of the left hand. Now the right hand is on the club in its most natural position, the right-hand palm approximately parallel to the left-hand palm.

"WE TWO ARE ONE"

Annie Lennox wasn't thinking about the golf grip when she wrote "We Two Are One," but the message fits. It's important for both your hands to act as a single unit on the club, which means that—despite what you've read and heard in the past about the lead hand dominating, or the grip pressure in one hand being greater than the other—neither hand should be stronger than the other on the club.

To keep the hands working as a single unit, players over the years started interlocking or overlapping certain fingers, usually the pinkie of the right hand and the index finger of the left. But there have been a lot of great ball strikers, including a Canadian golfing genius named Moe Norman, who played with all ten fingers on the club.

No matter how long you've played, I recommend that you give the three most common grips—the interlocking, overlapping, and ten-finger grips—a try. Even if you've used the same grip for ten, twenty, or thirty years, I believe you should shake it up and hold the club differently for a month or two. Not only will you become more aware of how you put your hands on the golf club, you will develop a greater understanding of the role the grip plays in establishing a foundation for the rest of your golf swing.

Two of golf's greatest performers, Jack Nicklaus and Tiger Woods, use the interlocking grip. However, their interlocking positions, like those of most good players who opt for this grip, lock or connect the right pinkie and left index finger more toward the nail than the base of the fingers. This is important, because if the

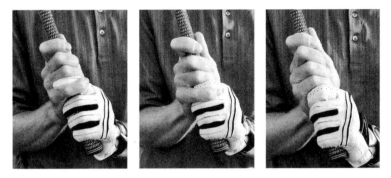

The three standard grip options.

two fingers are interlocked at their bases, tension increases and the handle of the club will tend to move up into the palm of the right hand, a position that gives many golfers the impression of playing tug-of-war—instead of holding an instrument designed for precise work.

"WITH MY ONE GOOD ARM BEHIND MY BACK"

Okay, I know Lou Reed didn't play golf when he wrote the preceding lyrics, but the one-arm-behind-my-back reference provides a great visual for one of the best drills in golf.

To find the grip that works best, you have to do a little experimenting. So take an 8-iron to the driving range and hit balls off a tee with only your left hand. *Note:* All these references are for right-handed players, since they encompass the vast majority of players. Lefties, as they are accustomed to doing, need to reverse all hand, feet, and side references. With that bit of business out of the way, head back to hitting balls with one hand, focusing on the grip you need to control the club and square the face at impact.

If you've never tried hitting balls with one arm before, be warned: you will whiff a few, and you will likely stick the club in the ground behind the ball a few times. When you do make contact, the shots are likely to squirrel off to the right or left until you get the hang of it.

Don't get frustrated; every whiff, squib, and shank is part of the learning process. Just as toddlers learn about the complicated kinesthetic and biomechanical process of walking each time they fall, golf tasks like hitting balls with only the left arm teach you more about clubface control than any intellectual exercise you can go through.

Not only will you find yourself instinctively modifying your grip to square the clubface and find the correct clubhead path, your brain will process that information faster and make the necessary adjustments quicker and more efficiently than it would if you were following step-by-step instructions from a book. Your focus again will be more on the what (squaring the clubface at impact), rather than the how-to (left-hand knuckles here, right elbow there, etc.).

Once you feel comfortable with the left-hand grip, put your left hand on your chest and hit balls with only your right hand on the club. If you are right-handed, you may find this a bit easier, especially if you have played any racket or paddle sports in the past. The whiffs may be plentiful, as may be the cold-tops and shanks. But don't get discouraged. There is no failure

Christopher hitting balls with left arm only, right arm at his side.

per se, only phenomenal feedback, so be patient. Once you reach a point where you can square the clubface and make contact with your right hand only, you will have found the perfect grip for you.

And find it you must. Picasso said, "You cannot teach painting, you must find it." The same can be said for holding a golf club. You must find what works best for you; good coaching and instruction can accelerate your exploration and learning process.

Christopher hitting balls with right arm only, left hand on chest.

"TRAPPED INSIDE THIS TWISTED MIND"

I figured I'd throw a little Foo Fighters in the mix to round out the foursome with Annie Lennox, Lou Reed, and Buck Owens. But like all the other lyrics I've pulled out of my eclectic reservoir, this one has a point.

Once you get a feel for the proper grip, you should walk away from the golf course, go into a room, and do nothing but put your hands on the golf club, hold the club for several seconds, take them off, and repeat. I prefer a room where there are no distractions: no TV, no radio, no pictures, and no people. A padded cell is optimal. I want all your focus to be on placing your hands on the club. With all your attention on only one thing, you will learn that single thing faster and more effectively than if there were other distractions.

The problem most people have with the basics is not that they haven't taken the time to learn them; rather, they think they've learned all there is to know about the fundamentals before they actually have. Sure, you can spend ten minutes on the mechanics of the grip and say, "I've got it." But you don't have it. Your rational brain might understand the mechanics of the process, but you haven't actually learned anything.

If you are of a certain age, you probably remember the movie *The Karate Kid.* One of the best scenes in that film is when Pat Morita makes Ralph Macchio wax his car and paint his fence, focusing on the circular motion of the waxing—"wax on; wax off"—and the long brushstrokes for painting. After days of this, Macchio gets fed up and says, "Enough." Then Pat tries to attack him, and Ralph defends himself instinctively by using the same motions he's been perfecting through waxing and painting.

Most of my students have the same reaction when I take them into an empty banquet room for a lesson on the grip. But it is only through painstaking repetition—left hand on the club; then right hand on; hold; release; repeat—that your brain and body actually learn the grip in a way that becomes instinctive.

Christopher teaching someone the grip in an empty banquet room.

Any form of distraction or interference—a swing, ball, or result—will retard the mastering and learning process.

You might know how to paint a fence, but you aren't ready to take on a black belt in karate. You might also know, intellectually, how to grip a golf club, but until you practice it in the confines of a quiet room with no distractions and nothing else on your mind, you will never perfect the most basic fundamental in golf.

"I CUT A PIECE OUT OF YOU"

To assume you are going to perfect the grip in one or two practice sessions would be like assuming you could take up jogging on Monday and win the New York Marathon on Saturday. Neither is going to happen.

The grip tasks outlined in this chapter will speed up the learning process. But you can also build your own teaching aid, which will serve as a guide to keep you from falling back into old habits.

To do this, take either an old golf club or one of the clubs in your bag that you don't hit very often, and grip it correctly. Once you are comfortable with your hand position, take a marker and put Xs on the spots where your thumbs fall. Then take a small knife and carve out notches in the grip so that the pads of your thumbs will fit in the grooves.

This kind of preformed grip is illegal in USGA competitions, so if you're planning on playing in the U.S. Open, you will have to take your grip-aid club out of play, or spend six dollars to get it regripped. For the rest of you, this club will serve as a guide—a periodic checkpoint—to advance your learning process and get you gripping the club the way you should.

WHAT YOU CAN LEARN FROM SPEED GOLF

I cringe whenever I see amateur players go through a contrived routine to grip the club. It happens more often than you realize. I'm sure you've seen friends or playing partners pull a club and start their routine by gripping the club in the first knuckle of the bottom three fingers of the left hand. Then they check the position of their left thumb, and slowly put their index finger on as if they are pulling some imaginary trigger. A few seconds later, they repeat the process with the right hand, all the while forgetting that there is a ball and a target, and the object is to get one close to the other.

They haven't learned the grip, so in the heat of the battle when all that counts is getting the ball from point A to point B, they're worried about where the "V" on the bottom hand is pointing. How could the shot be successful with such scattered focus?

In speed golf I never think about my grip, because I don't have time. I wear dry-fit gloves to wick away the perspiration, and after running to my ball, I grip the club I've chosen without wasting a second. I can only do this because holding a golf club correctly has become second nature, as intuitive to me as running. I don't have to think about putting one foot in front of the other and propelling myself from heel to toe as I run; nor do I have to think about where my left thumb or right index finger should be on the club. Because I took the time to learn the grip and it is now instinctive, I spend no more time thinking about putting my hands on the club than I do thinking about how to run.

Plus, in competitive speed-golf events, the outcome can come down to a few measly seconds. I've won and lost events by less than a minute, so saving time is critical. If I shoot 72 and take five seconds on each shot to verify my grip, I've lost six minutes.

If I'm really struggling to put my hands on properly, I could take ten seconds per shot and lose twelve minutes. I might as well be running uphill the whole time.

In traditional golf, you may not have to worry so much about the seconds lost. But if you are spending precious energy on your grip, it is taking your focus away from golf's essential concern: where and how you want the ball to go.

You didn't learn to walk in a day, and you won't learn to grip the golf club correctly in a day or two, either. But in committing the time and energy to the tedious and oh-so-vital task of learning the proper grip, you will shorten the time it takes to improve your game and cut down on the number of compensatory flaws in your golf swing that stem from a poor grip.

So many setup and in-swing faults are caused by a poor grip, yet far too often in golf we tend to address the effects rather than the causes. A poor grip creates a clubface that is not square at impact, which then leads to an improper swing path, followed by faulty body motion to compensate. So take the time and master a grip that produces a square clubface at impact. It will prevent many woes in the future.

THREE

O O O

"Don't Just Stand There"

During his heyday, Stevie Ray Vaughn had to play certain songs standing up. Something about the licks in "Voodoo Chile" forced the great guitarist to his feet. Sit him down with an acoustic Gibson, and he could still play, but the song lost its feel. Even if the audience couldn't see him, certain tunes had to be performed. Stevie had to move to make the music in order for the music to move him.

Sports are like that as well. Feed Shaquille O'Neal the basketball anywhere in the paint and he can hit a turnaround, jump hook, finger roll, or thunder dunk nine times out of ten. Put him on the foul line, where he has plenty of time and nowhere to move his feet, and making the shot becomes a fifty-fifty proposition.

When do you see a professional shortstop bobble the ball? It's not when he's making a diving play or a backhanded grab; it's when the ball is hit right to him and he doesn't have to move. And how many times have you seen an NFL receiver run a short route, plant his feet, and drop a pass that hits him right in the hands?

Just as the golf ball being static fights our instinct to chase a moving object, the fact that golf is played from a standing, not a running or reacting, position sends all kinds of conflicting signals to your brain. You tell yourself, "Wow, there the ball is, just sitting there. Now I'm supposed to plant my feet, take a stance, aim my body and the club where I want the ball to go, and hit it. That hardly seems fair. Shouldn't I get a running start or something?"

Because golfers do, indeed, plant their feet and assume a stance over the golf ball before swinging, most tie themselves in knots. You've seen them ticking off their mental checklists—feet shoulder-width apart, weight on the balls of the feet, left arm straight, right arm tucked, knees flexed, butt out, left hip higher than the right, chin up, bow at the waist, tilt spine angle to the right. The list is endless. Three thoughts into the process, this person is so contorted that making anything resembling a golf swing is impossible.

Setting up to hit a golf ball is not that physically demanding—you don't have to put your feet behind your ears or stand on your head—but golfers have a hard time getting into position because they are under no time constraints and they aren't reacting to anything. The only exception is speed golf. I've got no time for any sort of checklist. I've either learned the setup prior to arriving at the first tee, or I haven't.

If I throw a golf ball at one of my students, he or she will either raise a hand to catch it, or move quickly out of the way to dodge it. The one thing the student will not do is think about either of those motions. They are reflex reactions. The conscious brain doesn't say, "Okay, here comes a ball. Lift your left hand twenty inches and bend your elbow at a forty-degree angle, pronating the forearm and opening the fingers so the palm is facing the oncoming object," even though that is exactly what your body does. It has become an instinctive act through experience and successful repetition. That's where you are trying to get with your golf swing.

If you can go through such a complex series of motions to catch a ball thrown in your direction when the only thought shooting through your brain is "Oh, no, here comes a ball!" why can't you set up to hit a golf shot without thinking about it?

The answer is: there is no urgency. You've got all day. No rush. Might as well take your time, analyze every square inch of your body, and make sure everything is dead-letter perfect.

In addition, the whole act of striking a golf ball is a bit too easy. According to Dr. Marquardt, "The task of hitting a ball is too simple, so you start interacting mentally with thoughts of how to do it. It is much more complicated for the brain to organize how to hit static targets than moving ones." That might be the only thing easy about hitting one of Roger Clemens's fastballs.

To further illustrate how wrongheaded this process is, try thinking about every muscle you use and every motion you make when you're brushing your teeth. Focus on the hand you use to hold the toothbrush as the paste is applied. Then check your grip as you raise the brush to your mouth. How is your body positioned over the sink? Are you leaning forward? If so, are you bending at the waist or slumping from the shoulders? And what is the angle of your head? At what point do you rotate the brush so that bristles meet teeth? What muscles do you use to get those hard-to-reach areas behind the molars?

Once you have finished analyzing every motion required in something this rudimentary, you should realize how absurd it is to go through a similar checklist when you're setting up to hit a golf ball.

"But hold on," you say. "I brush my teeth every morning. I don't hit golf balls every day." Agreed, correct repetition—and a lot of it—is vital to learning to hit a golf ball, with or without coaching or instruction. And, you might add, "Hitting a golf ball is more complicated than brushing your teeth." Perhaps, but learning to strike a golf ball is no different neurologically for the brain than learning to brush your teeth, comb your hair, eat a bowl of cereal, or even walk or talk. The setup in golf is certainly a lot simpler than the complex motions required to clean your teeth. And the setup is just as individual as your toothbrush.

"NOBODY'S RIGHT—NOBODY'S WRONG"

Ben Hogan stood about five feet, eight inches and weighed 145 pounds. George Archer was six-six and a shade north of 200 pounds. Craig Stadler topped the scales at 260 pounds on his five-ten frame, and Tiger Woods is six feet two inches, 210 pounds. Michelle Wie is six-one, weight undisclosed (why would you ask?), while Jeong Jang, a past women's British Open winner, has to stand on her toes to touch the five-foot mark. Given their physical differences, it's obvious that all of these players set up to the golf ball differently. If Archer had tried to mimic Hogan's setup, he would have had a hard time getting the club on the ground behind the ball; Stadler might want to set up like Tiger, but there's the little problem of an expanded midsection getting in the way; and Jeong Jang and Michelle Wie set up so differently they might as well be playing a different game.

Those aren't the only examples of different setups. Byron Nelson stood over his shots with hunched, rounded shoulders, while Adam Scott works hard to keep his upper back perfectly straight, as if he were holding a grapefruit between his shoulder blades. Bobby Jones set up with his feet slightly less than shoulder-width apart, while Moe Norman took such a wide stance he looked like a clean-and-jerk weight lifter. Jack Nicklaus stood so close to the ball his arm hung straight down, and Gary Player stood so far away from it that he had to reach out like a sailor pulling a tie line.

All of those players set up in ways that allowed them to make comfortable, efficient, and effective golf swings. They couldn't have cared less if their setups mimicked those of the greats who came before them, because all those guys set up differently as well. As U.S. Open winner Geoff Ogilvy put it, "The best player in the world at one time never copies anyone else. But every generation of golfers copies the best golfer in the world at that time."

Just as the purpose of golf is to get the ball from the tee into the hole in as few shots as possible, the purpose of your setup is the following:

- Position the club and body in the fashion that best works for you and is conducive to hitting the intended shot.

- Free up the hands and arms so that you can square the clubface at impact and swing the clubhead on the desired path.

- For most full swings, place your body in an optimal position, in accordance with your physical capabilities to generate maximum clubhead speed at the moment of impact.

If you can accomplish those things by standing on one foot and spinning like a ballerina, then that's the setup that's right for you, although I wouldn't recommend it.

The point is, your setup will be different from that of almost everyone you know, because your body is different; your abilities are different; and the way you are likely to swing the golf club is different.

My students are constantly asking things like, "Christopher, do you believe in keeping both feet perpendicular to the target line, or do you think you should turn the feet out at an angle?" or "Christopher, are you an elbows-in or an elbows-out kind of teacher?" It sounds like a cop-out, but I believe in all those things and none of those things: it depends on the individual.

The same is true for alignment. I'm always asked: "Do you believe in a perfectly square alignment or in hitting the ball from a slightly open or slightly closed stance?" The truth is: I couldn't care less! If it works for you, do it. When Hall of Famer Larry Nelson was preparing for majors, John Gerring, the teaching pro at Atlanta Country Club at the time, would walk out and say, "Larry, I know you're ready, because I have no idea where you're aiming." Lee Trevino played his entire career lining up at least twenty yards left of his target, while Henrik Stenson, one of the top players in the world, lines up right and pulls every shot back on line. Putting wizard and British Open winner Bobby Locke aimed far right as well and hooked everything, putts included.

"Okay," you say, "but you have to have some guidelines. You don't line up ninety degrees away from your target."

Well, you do if you're trying to hit a ninety-degree cut, or a smother hook around a tree, just as Tiger can hit a punch-cut 2-iron that slices a hundred yards and never gets more than head-high, and Jack Nicklaus, who played a fade throughout his career, could hook the ball around Ike's Tree on the seventeenth at Augusta National every time he played the hole. Players develop their setups and alignments to complement what they are trying to do with the golf ball, and they adjust those setups depending on the shots they need to hit.

"FINDING THE ONE THAT I COULD FALL INTO"

Most teachers tell students that the golf setup is an athletic stance, no different from the one you use to hit a baseball, shoot a foul shot, or ski down a mountain. While there is a lot of truth to that, it doesn't do you a lot of good if you've never skied, played H-O-R-S-E in the backyard, or looked at a three-two fastball on the inside corner of the plate.

For those who wouldn't know an athletic stance from athlete's foot, there are a few games you can play to find the setup that is right for you—that is, the one that will allow you to make a good golf swing without the unnecessary mental checklists and game-killing physical contortions.

"FOLLOW THE BOUNCING BALL"
Posture

Find a ball around your house that you can bounce on the floor without hurting yourself or anyone else—a basketball, volleyball, soccer ball, or even a tennis ball. Then bounce the ball in front of you and catch it with both hands. Now bounce it and catch it as many times as you can in one minute, bouncing it quickly without losing control.

When you catch the ball the final time, check your posture. More than likely, you will have your feet somewhere near shoulder-width apart—maybe a little wider or a little narrower, but pretty close—and you will be bending forward from the waist with your weight on the balls of your feet. Your hands will be in front of you and your eyes will be on the ball. This is the same athletic posture you would assume if you were playing cornerback for the New England Patriots, shooting a game-winning foul shot in the Final Four, or, in your case, setting up to hit a golf shot.

To advance the game, put a golf club within easy reach, and after bouncing and catching the ball as many times as possible in your one minute, toss the ball aside and grab the golf club as if you were about to hit a shot. Do this quickly without changing your posture. The less time you devote to thinking about the setup, the more likely you are to assume the setup position that is right for you. You might feel as if someone is going to come and knock you off balance and you want to hold steady.

Once you have played this game with yourself a few times, try it in front of a full-length mirror. Mirrors and windows are fantastic learning tools, as they allow you to actually see what you are doing, as opposed to relying on what you may feel like or think you are doing. *Feel* is not real, but seeing yourself assuming an athletic posture helps build mental pictures that you can then take with you onto the golf course. It also helps you develop an awareness of what your individual setup looks like.

Close your eyes from time to time (this will help you to become better aware of your body in space). Then open them to verify your posture.

You'll probably be surprised. You don't look half bad.

"COMING DOWN SLOW WITHOUT A THING TO SHOW"
Ball Position

Nobody told Johnny Cash to play his guitar in front of his chest, just as nobody taught Pete Townshend to windmill his low-riding Fender Telecaster just above his knees. These Hall of Fame musicians played their instruments where and how they were most comfortable.

You should do the same when it comes to figuring out where and how to position your body in relation to the ball. How far away from the ball you should stand and where you should position the ball between your feet (front of your stance, middle of your stance, or more toward your back foot) depend a lot on how you swing the club and what setup is most natural for you. The lesser of the two evils in golf would be standing a bit closer to the ball than farther away with the ball positioned slightly forward in the stance rather than back, but, again, this is very individual— for both the player and the shot at hand.

To find out where the golf ball fits into this whole setup picture, try standing erect and holding a club straight out in front of you; now swing the club as if you were hitting a ball that was waist-high. Repeat the process, but move the club down a little as if the ball you were hitting was knee-high. Then swing the club just a few inches above the ground. And finally, swing the club as if the ball were on the ground. Wherever the club brushes the top of the ground is about where you should play the ball in relation to your stance.

This will vary, depending on the club and on the impact condition you are trying to create—and, of course, your own individual swing. In general, if you are trying to produce a slightly downward blow, where the club hits the ball first and then clips the grass or takes a divot, as with a short- or mid-iron, position the ball more toward the center of your stance; if you want the club to bottom out and hit the ball and grass/ground at about the same spot, as with a longer iron, hybrid, or fairway metal, move the ball a bit more forward; and, if you are trying to create a slightly upward strike on the ball, as with a driver, the ball must be played even more forward in the stance.

Repeat this game until you feel comfortable assuming this natural stance every time you step up to a golf shot, remembering that the faster you play this game, the more likely you are to react to your natural posture and optimal ball position.

Christopher making swings at different heights.

"ARE YOU GONNA GO MY WAY?"
Aim and Alignment

The great teacher Claude Harmon used to tell his students, "If you aim at nothing, you're always going to hit it."

The biggest problem I see with students who can't align themselves is that they focus on the ball instead of the target. It all starts with the eyes, as do most actions we undertake as humans. If you are worried about playing the ball off your left heel, and setting up with your head tilted behind the ball, your left shoulder higher than your right, and the sweet spot of the club positioned directly behind the ball, you most certainly are not paying much attention to the target. I can't tell you the number of students I have taught who take one cursory glance at the target and spend the rest of their preshot time staring at the ball, as if they had found some miraculous way of communicating telepathically with it to tell it where to go. Trying to hit a golf shot after this sort of preshot ritual is like shooting a basketball without looking at the hoop or throwing a football without looking at your receiver. Chances of success are pretty slim.

In golf we call this being "ball bound," a syndrome where the player locks in on the ball to the exclusion of virtually everything else, including the spot where you want the ball to end up after the shot. When the eyes become fixated on the ball, or inactive in general, the conscious mind begins to race. In order for aiming and aligning to become as second-nature to you as walking, you have to overcome your ball-bound anxiety and focus on moving the ball to a target. Learn which ball position and distance are most functional for you, often accomplished through trial and error on the practice tee, so that when it's time to play, you can advance the ball to the target as simply as you drive your car from home to work.

WHAT YOU CAN LEARN FROM SPEED GOLF

Speed golfers aim every shot; we just don't take much time doing it. But then again, when I ask someone to throw a ball at something, they don't take much time either. Most of my preshot analysis, including how far I am from the hole, what club I'm going to hit, the shape of the shot I need, and where I need to aim to achieve the desired result, occurs as I'm running to the ball. By the time I reach the ball, all the decisions have been made. I take a few moments to select a club, catch my breath, take a look or two, and fire. The whole process takes five to ten seconds, and that limited routine doesn't allow my ever-interfering conscious mind to get going.

This is possible because I don't worry about where my feet are pointing or whether my shoulders and hips are pointing on a parallel line to the target. I pick the spot where I want the ball to land, visualize the shot, set up, and swing. I've learned through practice and repetition where my body needs to be; my subconscious brain does the rest.

Fortunately, I have hit enough balls in my life to have confidence that I'm going to set up and aim correctly without thinking about it. If you play the preceding games, you will eventually achieve that same level of confidence.

○ ○ ○

FOUR

"Let's Get It Started"

Starting the swing correctly is a difficult thing, even for great players. The biggest problem is an overactive brain, which can paralyze any golfer and ruin the best golf swing even before it starts.

Hundreds of thoughts swirl through your mind before you swing. Some include:

- Where is my weight?

- Boy, I've really got to get this one up in the air.

- Who's watching me? Man, this is embarrassing.

- I've got to use my one-piece, swing-the-handle, pronate-the-forearms takeaway.

- What is my swing plane going to be?

- What am I doing here?

- Oh, God, where am I lined up?

- Is there trouble down the left side? Or out-of-bounds to the right? Or both?

- Don't leave it short!

These are the equivalent of brain hiccups: Tourette-like mental twitches that gum up the golf swing before any motion begins. If you've watched any golf on television, you've probably seen this. A player hits a bad shot in a pressure situation and the talking-head announcer says, "I saw a lot of indecision in that swing." Of course, the swing looked no different to you, and in all likelihood it didn't look that different to the analyst. What was "indecisive" was the preswing/preshot, the routine or pattern that the player normally used to get things started. Instead of grabbing the club out of the bag with confidence, taking two waggles while staring down the target, and swinging away, the player might have pulled one club, taken a practice swing, put the club back, pulled another one, taken another couple of practice swings, and then waggled the club three or four times without looking at the target. Or maybe he chose one club and took the right number of waggles but hesitated, staring at the ball and standing motionless for a few extra seconds before swinging.

Both those scenarios are disastrous. If a Tour player takes twenty seconds to hit the ball after taking the club out of the bag (an interminable amount of time, in my opinion), that sequence should not vary more than a second, no matter what the situation. If, in the heat of a tournament, a Tour player starts taking forty seconds to pull the trigger, he is, as TV analysts say, "indecisive." I call this malady "getting stuck."

I don't have this extended-time issue in speed golf. With the shot I want to play in mind, I stand over the ball just long enough to slow my heartbeat and feel that I can make a golf swing without passing out, and off I go.

Billy Casper, winner of fifty-one PGA Tour titles, two U.S. Opens, and a Masters, would go so far as to put the club back in the bag and start his preshot routine over from the beginning if he was disrupted or simply didn't feel comfortable over the ball.

Getting stuck can take many forms. Steve Sax, the Dodgers and Yankees second baseman, was the National League Rookie of the Year and a five-time All Star. But then, out of the blue, he got the yips and couldn't throw the ball to first base, a throw he'd made millions of times in his life. Somehow, he became so anxious and self-conscious about the mundane act of throwing the ball to first that he threw the ball in the stands. His throws became so bad that people who had season tickets behind first base started showing up in catcher's equipment.

The same thing happened to Chuck Knoblauch of the Yankees. His throws to first got so bad that he hit Keith Olbermann's mother in the head with a ball. Mackey Sasser, catcher for the Mets, woke up one morning and could no longer throw the ball back to the pitcher. He tried. He made the motion with his throwing arm, but when it came time to release the ball, Mackey couldn't let go. It got so bad that he had to walk the ball back to the pitcher.

Did Sasser, Knoblauch, and Sax forget how to throw a baseball? Of course not. Just like the Broadway actor who performs the same play two times a day, six days a week, for a year doesn't forget his lines, even when he forgets his lines, and professional musicians don't forget the words to songs they themselves wrote, even when they do. Everyone has mental spasms, those moments when you can't recall the name of your best friend's spouse, whom you've known for years, or you forget the words to your favorite song, a tune you've sung since you were a kid. For most, those moments are fleeting. You get frustrated or embarrassed for a minute or two, and then remember what you knew all along. It is only when the mental hiccup turns into a full-fledged, debilitating syndrome—as it did for Sasser, Knoblauch, and Sax—that it becomes a problem.

As Phil Lee, a noted psychiatrist and medical doctor, says: "It's no different from someone who turns off the toaster by rote, walks out one morning, and says, 'Gosh, did I turn it off this morning?' He gets out of his car and goes back inside to check, even though he turns the toaster off every morning and there is no logical reason to believe this morning was any different. As long as that is a one-time thing, it's no big deal, a mental blip; we all have them. But when you turn off the toaster, walk out, convince yourself you didn't, walk back in, check it, walk back out, convince yourself again that you didn't, walk back in, and repeat that process dozens of times, you are in obsessive-compulsive mode."

Some golfers get stuck to a point where they can't start the swing at all. For a while, the most pronounced mental tic in professional golf belonged to Sergio García. In late 2000, Sergio developed a habit of regripping (milking) his grip prior to takeaway. By 2001, the habit had evolved into an annoying mental stutter, and by the summer of 2002, it was a full-blown disorder. He would stand over the ball milking, and milking, and milking the grip, sometimes for as long as twenty seconds before starting the swing. It got so bad that at the 2002 U.S. Open the New York fans in the gallery at Bethpage Black (not a meek bunch) began counting Sergio's regrips out loud. They got to nineteen before a marshal intervened. Thankfully, Sergio cured this spasm and is back to a consistent and reasonably time-conscious routine.

You can eliminate the problem before it starts by practicing/playing a few simple games to help you start your golf swing correctly.

"YOU ARE THE APPLE OF MY EYE"

Am I the only one who laughed when Stevie Wonder sang that line?

We know Stevie never played golf, even though there are plenty of outstanding blind golfers, but the point of the line for our purposes is that the eyes hold the key to how active or inactive the brain is prior to the golf swing. The rule of thumb is

Active eyes = passive brain
Passive eyes = active brain

You know this to be true. How many times have you seen a member of your foursome stand over a shot as if he had turned to stone? The eyes don't move—heck, nothing moves! Now think about how many times that person hit a perfect shot after locking in on the ball and standing perfectly still. It doesn't happen often. In fact, when you see someone stare at the ball without moving for more than a second or two, you instinctively know he isn't going to hit it well.

When the eyes are active (between ball and target), the mind is passive; conversely, when the eyes are passive (stuck staring at the ball), the mind is filling with swing thoughts.

In speed golf, I'm intensely focused on my target and only have a vague realization that the ball is there at all. I'm much more interested in the destination—the target—than the inanimate sphere at my feet. Much like driving a car: you're not looking at the steering wheel or gas pedal; you are looking at where you're going.

The best players spend most of their preshot time looking somewhere other than at the ball. Some look at their hands, and then at their feet, and then at the target, while others just look at where they want the ball to go. Hubert Green used to look back and forth between the ball and the target so many times that he looked like he might get whiplash before swinging the club. Short-game maestro and two-time Masters winner José María Olazábal does the same.

The one common denominator among all these players is that they spend a minimal amount of their preshot time looking

Christopher staring at his target while waggling a club.

at the ball. Tiger Woods is the best in the world at this (along with being the best at every other aspect of the game). From the time he grips the club in his right hand and starts his preshot routine from behind the ball until he makes contact, Tiger spends almost all of his time staring at the target. The eyes move back and forth between the target and the ball a couple of times, and his eyes don't turn exclusively to the ball until he is ready to begin his swing.

There are no paralyzing swing thoughts going through Tiger's brain while he stares down his target; there are no mental hiccups disrupting his routine, no anxieties freezing him in place. Whether he is hitting a shot in the U.S. Open or in a Monday afternoon match at his home club in Florida, Tiger's routine never changes, and his eyes never lock in on the golf ball until the swing is under way.

Jack Nicklaus's eyes panned from his ball to the target and then back to the ball: a linear approach to keeping the eyes busy so as to quiet the mind. To eliminate your own mental anxiety and stop the paralysis before it starts, work on keeping the eyes active until the second the swing begins.

Try this little trick Doc Farnsworth taught me years ago: pick out two objects in the distance that are not next to each other, like a tree and a flagstick. Begin to move your eyes between the objects. Then, little by little, increase the speed at which your eyes move back and forth, until it is quite rapid. What's going on in your mind as you do this? Nothing. Your brain is calm and quiet: the perfect mind state in which to hit a golf shot.

As we near the moment to pull the trigger—start the swing—there are a variety of ways to get the motion started. Most good players have a minimove that triggers the swing. These can initially take the form of swing thoughts, until rehearsed enough that they become second nature. Like most everything in golf, you need to find the trigger that works best for you. This is accomplished through trial and error and competent coaching and instruction. Here are a few that may be floating around the swing-thought storage area of the brain:

- Waggle the club like Tiger, Mike Weir, Tom Watson—or perhaps not at all, like Seve.

- Bounce the clubhead on the ground behind the ball.

- Forward-press the hands.

- Shuffle your feet once . . . twice . . . three times a golfer.

- Cock the head to the right à la Jack Nicklaus (works particularly well for left-eye-dominant people).

- Kick your right knee toward the target like Gary Player and Sam Snead.

These triggers are not wrong; in fact, they work great for the major champion winners listed. But those guys don't bounce the club, shuffle their feet, or waggle the club just to do it. Their goal (and yours) is to get the swing started in a smooth, fluid, and orderly fashion, free of tension. Tension loves stillness, so keep something moving—eyes, arms, club, feet, or some combination thereof.

Interestingly enough, most swinging motions start with a micromove in the same direction. If you were to throw a bucket of water on someone, your first move would actually be a tiny move toward the victim, then you'd pull the bucket back before swinging it forward for the dousing. Standing motionless with the bucket doesn't produce the best result, just as staring at the ball before swinging a golf club is a recipe for disaster.

"YOU GOTTA START SMALL"

Because the backswing is the first verse of the golf swing, it naturally influences the outcome of the shots. If you start the first few bars of a song off-key, it's almost impossible to recover. If you botch the backswing, the chances of making decent contact are slim to none.

It is also impossible for me, or any other golf instructor, to tell you how to take the club back in a way that applies to everyone. Oh, plenty have tried. A few of the more creative suggestions for the takeaway include:

- Push the clubhead back, initiating the movement with the middle deltoid muscle of the left shoulder.

- Pull the club back by turning the back of your right hand toward your right thigh.

- Initiate a one-piece takeaway by keeping the triangle formed by your arms and an imaginary vector between your left and right shoulder intact as you rotate on an imaginary axis just behind your sternum.

- Swing the handle, not the clubhead.

- Swing the clubhead, not the handle.

- Keep the clubface looking at the ball for the first foot or so.

- Allow the clubface to rotate (open) as it starts away from the ball.

- Keep the club low to the ground for eighteen inches, and then begin the upward ascent by rotating the hands and cocking the wrists until a ninety-degree angle is formed between your left arm and the shaft of the club.

- Sweep the club back away from the ball on a curved arc that bends toward a spot behind your right foot.

Ball striker extraordinaire Moe Norman was told early on in his career that most of the faults that occur in the golf swing take place in the first twelve to eighteen inches. Moe had a simple way to deal with this—he simply started with the clubhead twelve inches or so behind the ball.

If you are more into visuals for "how to" take the club away, consider these three examples, all based on phenomenal players.

- Miller Barber (this motion works well to start a lawn mower as well)
- Jim Furyk (the beginning of the "octopus in a phone booth" swing, as David Feherty once called it)
- Raymond Floyd (if Raymond's tailbone was up against a mirror, he'd break the mirror with the clubhead in the first few instants of the swing)

And at the top of the backswing, try a few of these on for further confusion:

- Never let your hands get higher than your right shoulder.

- Make sure your hands are high at the top.

- Get maximum separation between your hands and the ball at the top.

- Keep your right arm tucked close to your right side at all times.

- Rotate your head to the right (away from the ball) as the club reaches the top of the swing.

- Keep your head still.

- Move the torso laterally to the right if necessary to ensure that the left shoulder turns completely behind the ball.

- Rotate on an axis with no lateral shift.

- Let the left heel rise off the ground naturally at the top.

- Keep both feet on the ground.

- Turn the hips with the shoulders.

- Keep your hips still.

- Keep the left wrist cupped at the top.

- Always swing with a flat left wrist.

Earth-shattering, breaking news for all golf-publication subscribers: there is one thing all PGA Tour players have in common at the tops of their backswings: They all have shirts on.

Confused yet? You get the point. Not only could you never think about these things and make a golf swing, there is so much contradictory advice out there, you'd go crazy trying to sort through it all. My favorite was when I saw a guy tell his girlfriend that she needed to "wind up like you're at the plate waiting on a fastball."

Christopher hitting a ball off a tee with a very small swing.

The poor girl had never held a baseball bat in her life and was probably wondering if he meant a salad plate or dinner plate.

Like all other aspects of the golf swing, the takeaway is a very individual motion that you must discover on your own through exploration and repetition. No two takeaways—or swings, for that matter—will look alike, because no two individuals are alike physically, emotionally, or temperamentally. Both the takeaway and swing must be your own work of art and reflect a bit of your personality. Your fundamentals will be uniquely your own. The best way to begin that discovery process is to start small.

With the ball on a tee, an 8-iron in your hands, and in your normal address position for a full swing, make the smallest swing you can and still make contact. Try, literally, to fly the ball ten to twenty yards, focusing on nothing but striking the ball with the middle of the clubface.

If you hit the ground or top the ball off the tee, take less swing. Think smaller. This will get you moving the club back and forth through the hitting area in a way you can consistently repeat while making solid contact—and help you to find the way in which you swing the club back to create solid contact.

"LET YOUR LOVE GROW"

As you become comfortable making solid contact with a very small swing, try growing your backswing, keeping in mind that the purpose is to build a swing you can repeat consistently while making solid contact.

If you start mis-hitting shots, go back to your smaller swing. It's much like learning to ski. We all must start on the bunny hill before heading for the top of the mountain. So if you are unable to create good contact with a bigger swing, go back to the ten- to twenty-yard 8-irons off the tee (the bunny hill). It is far more important that the club meet the ball squarely than it is for you to make a long, looping backswing. If you have to play with a half-swing for a while, so what? Doug Sanders played for fifty years without ever getting his hands above hip-high, and Allen Doyle won back-to-back U.S. Senior Open titles with a backswing that looked as though he learned to play in a room with five-foot ceilings.

The problem most amateurs have is that they think they need to wind up and whack the ball with the biggest swing possible, since they've made reasonable contact a couple of times with a less-than-full swing. They figure they've "got it," since they've done it successfully a couple of times. That would be like taking the new skier to a World Cup downhill course in Switzerland after a couple of successful turns down the bunny hill.

If you played golf for the next six months taking nothing but half-swings and making dead-solid contact, your scores would go down, and you would build a repeatable takeaway that gets the club where you need it to be in order to strike the ball cleanly.

Christopher making a one-quarter backswing.

Christopher making a one-half backswing.

Christopher making a three-quarter backswing.

Christopher making a full backswing.

"SLOW HAND"

Once you feel comfortable that you are taking the club back in a way that allows you to make solid contact with the ball, you want to train your mind-body system to repeat that same backswing for every swing in every situation. Later on, you may find that you take the club back differently to hit different shots. Repetitive-motion specialists have figured out that the best way to develop that kind of consistent, grooved motion is not to focus on this or that swing thought but to develop the entire backswing comprehensively. The backswing (and the entire golf swing itself, for that matter) is an ever-developing puzzle, made up of many moving parts and angles, a geometry full of cause and effect. So to increase your ability to get physical feedback on your own, take the backswing learning process as slowly as possible.

Here's how to get started. Shoot some video—both face-on and side view—of yourself making the backswing that allows you to make solid contact, and use that as your model. Now print out a few stills of different positions in the backswing. Then head back to the padded cell where you learned your grip and set up; I'll let you put a mirror up now so you can begin to see what you're feeling. There is no need for a ball, driving range, or golf course to master your backswing, since those things will distract you from your learning.

Now mimic what you see in those printouts. That's you—finding your trigger, taking the club away, and making a backswing—in the way that works best for you.

Most of you will slow down the backswing to about one second, maybe one and a half seconds, on the first try. To perfect the motion, you need to slow it down to twenty to twenty-five seconds total, a pace so slow that you will feel as though you aren't moving at all, as though you're standing in a twelve-foot swimming pool full of honey.

It is one of the many ironies of golf that to speed up the learning process, you have to slow down the pace of your swing in practice. Remember, learning takes time. Douglas Fields, the director of the Laboratory of Developmental Neurobiology at the National Institutes of Health in Bethesda, Maryland, says, "Flicking switches is not how we learn a lot of things. Getting good at piano or chess or baseball takes a lot of time." But by taking the club back so slowly—and optimally for you—you ingrain the motion and begin to build the motor patterns that will allow you to make the desired swing thoughtlessly in the future. And by focusing all your attention on the backswing— no downswing, no ball flight, no result—you will learn your ideal motion in the most time-efficient manner.

"SING A SONG"

Getting stuck stems from an unhealthy fixation on a small piece of the puzzle instead of seeing the entire picture and enjoying it for what it is. That goes for golf, but it's true of other things as well. If you focus on the germs in the air instead of the beauty of a spring day, you will forever remain cooped up inside, afraid to venture beyond the nearest Lysol bottle. If you continually fear throwing the ball over the pitcher's head, even though you've made the same throw a million times, you will become so consumed by your fear that you can't let go of the ball. And if you fear screwing up a golf shot—hitting the ball in the water, topping it off the tee, hitting one of the houses on the right—then you will become paralyzed by those thoughts and be unable to make a decent golf swing. It is like getting in your car and focusing on what you don't want to do (run into the curb, another car, a pedestrian, etc.). Pay attention and take keen interest in where you want to hit the golf ball, not on where you don't want to hit it.

To lighten your mind and distract it away from all that negativity, try the same game we played while putting: hit balls while listening to the same song over and over. Only this time, I want you to actually sing the song as you hit practice balls. You might want to make sure you are alone on the range (or at least out of earshot of your fellow golfers), but you should sing along with the tune you pick to ensure that your mind is on the music and not on all the bad things that might happen if you miss a shot.

Lee Trevino was the best in the world at this. He won the British Open at Muirfield with Tony Jacklin and Jack Nicklaus nipping at his heels while singing a Tom T. Hall song. "God didn't make the little green apples / and it don't rain in Indianapolis / in the summertime." The BBC commentators chuckled at Trevino's carefree style (and his inability to carry a tune), but at the end of the tournament it was the Merry Mex who was the winner of the gold medal and Champion Golfer of the Year. Talking, or singing in this instance, quieted the mind and allowed Trevino's body to function according to how it had been trained.

WHAT YOU CAN LEARN FROM SPEED GOLF

Spending time over the ball raises a speed golfer's score, so the most preshot finagling you will ever see a speed golfer do is to waggle the club once or twice before going straight into his or her swing. And a practice swing is nothing but wasted time. Besides, practicing is for the practice tee or driving range, not the golf course. Never will you see a speed golfer standing over the ball without moving. Those few precious seconds could mean the difference between winning a tournament and not placing. Because speed golfers never stop moving, they never have time to tense up, and they never give themselves the opportunity to develop a preshot brain tic.

That doesn't mean we don't have struggles and anxieties. Speed golfers go through the same struggles as everyone else. But we minimize how those challenges affect our games by simply eliminating the time it takes to dwell on them. Less is more. I certainly don't have time in a round of golf that takes less than an hour to be fiddling with my takeaway. What goes on before the motion begins and in the backswing must be mastered before arriving at the first tee, so all my attention can be on where I'm trying to send the little white ball—nothing else. You will play better if you adopt a similar approach.

FIVE

O O O

"Sweet Impact"

When King Hassan II of Morocco showed up for a golf lesson at Winged Foot, the renowned Westchester County, New York, golf club that has hosted many major championships, he did so with an entourage that approached a hundred people. His Highness was in town for a UN conference, but as a new golfer, he also wanted to get a few tips from Claude Harmon and play a round at one of the world's best golf clubs.

The lesson looked like a Tiger Woods clinic. So many people gathered around the tee that additional security had to be brought out to control the crowds. As famous as Winged Foot was, it wasn't every day that royalty visited.

After a couple of swings, Claude realized that, like most new golfers, the king was a little nervous hitting balls in front of such a large gallery. So, in typical Harmon fashion, Claude put his arm around the king and said, "Your Highness, that ball and club do not know you are the king of Morocco. They don't know, and they don't care. The only thing making that ball go is the club, and the only way the club is going to make it go where you want it to is through your swing. So, forget all this other stuff, and let's work on making the club meet the ball the way it should."

No better advice has ever been given.

I'm always surprised when people ask me, "Christopher, what's the most important position in golf?" as if golf is a series of statuesque poses that are judged like figure skating routines. It's like asking, "What's the most important note in a song?"

I always shake my head at the question and say, "Impact is the only thing that matters. Everything else—grip, setup, alignment, backswing, tempo, head position, spine angle, swing plane, and follow-through—is geared toward the nanosecond when club meets ball. Not only is it the most important position; impact is the only important position. Nothing else matters at all, period."

The ball and club don't know whether you're a twenty-eight handicapper or a club champion, whether you have five loops in your swing or a smooth, beautiful, Ernie Els kind of swing, the sort of thing people video and download to their "favorites" files on their computers. The ball doesn't know if you're fat, thin, short, tall, ugly, or destined for the cover of *People* magazine. In fact, the only thing the ball does is obey the laws of physics. It moves when it is struck by a club—"an object at rest remains at rest until acted upon by an outside force."

How the ball reacts to being struck by the club is also simple physics. A ball doesn't roll along the ground on its own, just as it doesn't curve thirty yards right or left on a whim. The angle at which the ball is struck, the speed of the club that is striking it, where on the club face (high, low, toe, heel, or sweet spot) the ball is struck, where the clubface is pointing, and the direction the clubhead is traveling when it makes contact all combine to determine how the ball will fly (or not) and where it will end up. And although all the golf ball knows is physics, each person will create those optimal physical elements at impact in his or her own unique and individual way.

By understanding the basics of where and how the club moves the ball, you will be able to develop a swing that allows you to apply the club optimally at the moment of impact, and, as a result, control where and how the ball travels to its target.

"I'D DRAW MYSELF GOING IN THE RIGHT DIRECTION"

Gnarls Barkley's lyrics perfectly illustrate an important point about impact and the golf swing in general. Too often, golfers have no idea why the ball flies a particular way, so they have no concept of how to adjust their swings in order to change their ball flight.

I can't tell you how many times I've seen players who align their bodies thirty yards left of the target, point the clubface thirty yards right of the target, and then become frustrated and confused when they hit a huge slice. "Gee, I made a great backswing, and felt like I delivered the club on an inside plane, all that stuff I've been reading in 'Cure Your Slice' magazines for years. Why does it still go right?"

First off, you do not hit the ball with your backswing. Sure, it's important for you to find the backswing that allows you to get to an ideal impact position, but the ball is not located somewhere behind your head. Making a perfect or esthetically pleasing backswing holds no guarantee for crisp ball contact (see Jim Furyk, Raymond Floyd, and Miller Barber). And, in the immortal words of Claude Harmon, "They call it golf—not pretty."

This common theme shows a complete ignorance of the general physical laws of golf. To avoid falling into that trap, you need to remember two crucial things:

- Where the clubface is pointing at impact is the overriding factor in where the ball goes. (Although this is influenced by clubhead speed and loft.)

- A golf ball only curves when the clubface does not match up with the path of the clubhead at the moment of impact.

In other words, if your shots start left and curve right, the clubhead is traveling on a leftward path when it hits the ball, and the clubface is pointing somewhere right of that path. If your shots start straight at the target but curve left, your clubhead is traveling straight down the target line at impact, but the clubface is pointing left at impact. And if your shots start right and go farther right, your clubface is traveling on a path that is to the right of the target, and the clubface is pointing even farther right. This is all assuming you are hitting the ball toward the center of the clubface; an improper clubhead path will affect where on the face you hit the ball. If you are striking the ball excessively toward the heel or toe, you will have a whole other plethora of possible ball flights.

The other important physical law that many people don't understand is that backspin makes the ball go up, and topspin makes the ball go down. So:

- A ball struck with a descending blow (the clubhead moving downward at impact) will spin up into the air.

- A ball struck with an ascending blow (the clubhead moving upward at impact) will have topspin and will not get airborne.

Golf is a game full of opposites, and the preceding law may be the greatest of all opposites. Remember, according to most historical experts, the game was invented by drunken Scottish shepherds whacking rocks to targets with sticks. Particularly for newer players, what makes a golf ball fly (or not fly) the way it does is extremely counterintuitive and illogical. Despite what your playing partners might tell you, a topped shot is not caused because you "didn't get under it" or you "lifted your head up." The ball fails to get airborne because you tried too hard to get under it and you flipped or scooped the club at the ball. This sent the leading edge of the clubhead—the bottom part of the clubface—crashing into the middle part of the ball (around the equator), creating an upward, glancing blow. The resulting topspin caused the ball to roll along the ground.

If you were to hit the top of the ball (which some of my students with more severe muscular coordination issues have done), the ball would carom into the ground, pop up, and hit you somewhere between the shin and forehead.

"GOT ME FEELIN' IT"

In another of the seemingly contradictory, 180-degree out-of-phase aspects of learning this silly game, in order to train your mind and body to control your ball flight, you have to first eliminate ball flight from your mental equation and focus on making solid contact with a full golf swing. So, if you have never hit a ball into a driving net, now is the time.

Putting a driving net in front of you does a couple of things. First, it eliminates the anxiety you feel when you're standing over a golf shot wondering if you're going to slice it, hook it, shank it, or top it. Second, it allows you to focus on aiming toward a spot that is right in front of you. You don't have to worry about hitting the ball hundreds of yards downrange, because the net is only a few feet in front of you. Pick a spot on the net, maybe a single square in the mesh or an area a few inches wide, make sure the clubface is pointing toward the small target, and focus on launching the ball, with solid contact, at the target. Draw a bull's-eye on a piece of paper and tape it to the back of the net if that helps. But do whatever it takes to focus on hitting the ball to a very small target only a few feet in front of you with a full swing. If you are unable to hit on or very near the small target while making good contact with a full swing, heed the advice from chapter 4 and go back to an easier, smaller swing in order to produce good contact and initial direction.

Christopher hitting balls into a net.

Finally, the net will allow you to concentrate on making solid contact, consistently returning the club to the ball so that you make clean, crisp hits imparting the proper amount of backspin and starting the ball in the intended direction.

This task will improve the consistency of your shots no matter what your skill level. You will also find that, once you eliminate ball flight from your mental equation, you will become more relaxed and confident with your swing, which will lead to more solid, long-flying shots.

"SLOW RIDE"

Nothing like a little Foghat reference when you're making a golf point. But just as you did with your backswing, you should use a mirror and a video camera to improve your impact position. Print out a picture of yourself in the optimal impact position (see below). Pose in that perfect impact spot for several seconds—as if someone is going to take your picture and send it into a major golf publication. Admire the angles and positions and—most important—begin to capture the overall feel of proper impact. Close your eyes for a few seconds.

Then rehearse putting the club and your body in the optimal position to create good impact—once again very slowly—with and without a golf ball. When you are in super-slow-motion practice mode, focusing on the ideal impact position, your ball might not even make it to the net. That's okay: you are simply trying to help your mind and body learn the feel and sensations that go along with correct impact.

During a practice round for the 2006 PGA Championship at Medinah Country Club, Tiger Woods hit nearly two dozen shots—with full swings—where the ball went only twenty to fifty yards. These were super-slow-motion swings, designed to help Tiger capture the appropriate feel of the swing he wished to produce. He performed these swings with a variety of clubs, including his driver, during a practice round for a major championship, with, as always, a generous gallery present. If Tiger is willing to go to such lengths to capture the necessary feel and build the desired motor pattern—on center stage—you must be willing to do the same at home in front of a mirror and into a net.

By the way, Tiger won that tournament by five shots.

When videotaping your full swing at full speed, if the ball contact is not crisp and you notice that the club and body are not in optimal positions at impact, go back to smaller and slower swings. Once again, the knowledge of where the club and body must be to produce crisp contact is not paramount to the execution; correct repetition is, whether that be with a less-than-full swing, in slow motion, or without a ball.

An ideal impact position.

"IS THIS ALL THERE IS?"

I can almost hear the cries now: "But Christopher, what about all those tips I've heard for years? I can't just start hitting shots into a net and get better, can I?"

By tips, you mean the ones like:

- The proper downswing sequence is shift (the weight), turn or rotate (the hips, then shoulders), then swing (the arms and club).

- Start the downswing by rotating the hips toward the target.

- "Bump" your hips toward the target to initiate the downswing.

- Push off with your right foot, shifting your weight to the left side as the club starts down.

- Drop the club onto a downswing plane that is inside your backswing plane.

- Keep your back to the target as you begin your downswing.

- Drop your right elbow against your right side on the downswing.

- Lag the clubhead behind the hands as long as possible prior to impact.

- Drive the knees down the target line.

- Pull the club down to the ball with the left arm.

- Keep the left wrist flat at impact—or the right wrist bent.

- Keep your head behind the ball at impact.

- Right heel down at impact.

- Right heel slightly raised at impact.

- Release the club at the bottom of the arc.

- Rotate the forearms so that the left palm is facing skyward and the right palm is facing the ground immediately after impact.

- Stand tall through impact.

- Maintain your spine angle through impact.

- Let the right shoulder lift your head after impact.

- Hit the ball hard with your right side and hand.

- Keep the back of the left hand moving down the target line as long as possible through the hitting area.

- Extend the right arm and club so that both point toward the target immediately after impact.

If you don't believe you can strike a golf ball cleanly without filling your mind with technical mumbo jumbo, then you should go to the range and think about all of the swing thoughts just listed. Especially when you consider that from the top of the backswing to impact takes about one-fifth of one second. Meanwhile, I'll have one of my students hit balls into a net with no other instruction than "Hit it solid, and focus on flying the ball into one small square in the back of the net," using nothing more than a picture in his head of what the club and body must look like at impact to produce solid contact. In a month, I'd bet my life savings on the guy with no swing thoughts and a lot of experience hitting solid shots.

"I LIKE THE WAY YOU MOVE ME, BABY"

To avoid falling back into old habits, make less-than-full swings with reduced energy and a lofted club. Once you have built some consistency with smaller, easier swings and short, lofted clubs, begin to make bigger, faster swings with longer, less-lofted clubs. In fact, the fastest way to learn, and gain confidence in your newfound natural golf swing, will be by adhering to the following guidelines:

- No more straight shots. Good players curve the ball—on purpose and with control—every time. Inconsistent, higher handicappers try and hit the ball straight. Straight in golf is a bogus and unrepeatable goal. Although with today's ball and club technology the ball flies straighter than ever, a straight ball is simply a good mis-hit. Tiger Woods has nine different possible ball flights, just for his driver. And while you are not Tiger Woods, you can learn to curve the ball and vary your trajectory with your small swings. The things you learn there will travel to your bigger, faster motions with less-lofted clubs.

- Stick with it. Now that you understand the physics of what makes a ball curve (the face and the path do not match up), you have to ingrain it through repetition and trial and error. Try curving the ball a lot, then curving it a little. If the ball accidentally curves the wrong or unintended way, don't worry, just exaggerate the feeling of the ball flight you are trying to produce. Once you have gained some competence in a particular ball flight and trajectory, go explore a new one.

Ben Hogan, one of the greatest ball strikers of all time and perhaps the game's most prodigious practice-tee master, would never put a club back in his bag during a practice session until he was confident—through dogged and determined practice—that he could consistently hit the intended shot. According to Jody Vasquez, Hogan's longtime ball shagger, caddy, and friend, and author of *Afternoons with Mr. Hogan*, the legendary player never went to the range with an agenda. "Mr. Hogan would hit the same club in practice until he felt confident he could produce the shot under pressure. If need be, he might spend the entire day practicing with the same club, hitting the same shot, until he got it right—to his standards."

It is also true that during a U.S. Open one year, Hogan's caddie was out shagging balls on the range when he lost the ball in the sun and was promptly hit in the head with an incoming 5-iron shot. The caddie staggered and fell to the ground, and before he could fully right himself, Hogan hit him in the head again.

You may discover that you are only truly confident with a single ball flight, let's say a medium-height ball that curves five to twenty-five yards from left to right. As much as you might try, the right-to-left shot doesn't seem to be in your repertoire. At this point you have two options: seek instruction and dedicate some time—or play with what you've got. Bruce Lietzke (left to right) and Allen Doyle (right to left) have made millions of dollars relying on a single ball flight that works for them. If that is what you are comfortable and confident with, "so it goes," as the late Kurt Vonnegut would say.

If you feel the need to curve the ball in different directions to shoot lower scores, find a competent coach and continue the learning experience. But there is nothing wrong with hitting one kind of shot as long as you can repeat it consistently. Knowing where the ball is going to go is a lot more important than your ability to work the ball in different directions. And controlling the golf ball is the end-all in golf, yet in order to do so, you must give up trying to control the swing with swing thoughts.

"PRACTICE MAKES PERFECT"

Once you have gained a certain amount of control of your golf ball through proper practice and repetition, you are ready to rehearse what you will face on the golf course. The kind of "bulk practice" I've suggested so far is essential for building the motor skills needed to hit a golf ball, but it doesn't have much to do with what transpires in a round of golf. Consider mixing in a few of the following ideas, which better simulate what actually happens on the course:

- Never hit the same shot twice. You won't on the golf course, so why do it on the range? If you have an 8-iron in your hand, try hitting one shot low and turning left, and with the next swing, try hitting a high one that turns left to right. Then hit one full, say 150 yards, with whatever ball flight you choose. Continue by hitting one that flies 125 yards, then one that goes 100 yards, another that goes 75, and another that goes 50, and finally one that only goes 25 yards, all with specific ball flights in mind. Try the same thing with a fairway wood, reducing your yardage by 25 yards with each swing. Although you may never hit a 50-yard 8-iron in a round of golf, this sort of practice helps to develop creativity, imagination, and feel—musts to hitting good golf shots. In addition, you will begin to master the nuances of impact—clubface angle, clubhead path, effective loft, angle of attack, and clubhead speed—that are necessary to control distance and ball flight. Practice this enough, and you will awaken the golf artist within you.

- Hit a variety of shots within the range that you will use a particular club, from different lies if possible. If you normally hit your 5-iron 170 yards, practice hitting shots of 160 to 175 yards, again with a variety of ball flights. This will more closely simulate what will be required on the golf course.

Christopher hitting a punch-cut 3-wood

- Play nine holes on the range. Visualize a nine- or eighteen-hole golf course layout that you know well. Then play that course from tee to green on the range. Picture each shot you would normally play, and then instead of immediately grabbing the club you would hit next, wait for five to ten minutes. If you were actually playing, you wouldn't hit your next shot twenty or thirty seconds after your first. You would wait for the others in your group to play, walk up the fairway, chat a little bit, then, a few minutes later, it would be your turn to play again. In reality, you would have waited several minutes between shots and arrived at your ball to find a completely different lie, likely using a completely different club. This practice scenario more closely resembles playing golf, but have you ever seen anyone do this?

By manipulating shots with every club, never hitting the same shot twice, and taking a few minutes between each swing, you train your mind to create golf shots and simulate a round of golf rather than working on the mechanics of a golf swing that you're most likely never going to repeat once you get on the course. Besides, as a creature of habit, if all you do is work on your golf swing when practicing, what do you think you'll do when you get on the golf course? Well, of course, you'll work on your golf swing. You won't miraculously be able to flip a switch and start to hit golf shots and *work the ball* during a round of golf if you haven't thoroughly rehearsed and learned those skills in your practice sessions.

Each shot you create provides your mind and body with critical feedback on clubface position and the path and speed of the clubhead when it makes contact with the ball—things you have to learn and understand if you are ever going to learn to "play golf" instead of "playing golf swing."

"RUSH, RUSH"

Okay, using a line from a Paula Abdul song might be a new low, but the game the lyrics could describe is great for developing your ability to hit golf shots instead of bogging yourself down with swing thoughts.

Tee up six balls in a line, three to four inches apart. Then pick a target somewhere down the range, a flag or a tree in the distance, but make sure the target is too far away to be reached with the club you have in your hand. If you're hitting a 5-iron, pick a spot 300 yards away; if you're hitting a driver, pick a tree or a house somewhere beyond the 400-yard mark.

Now hit each ball as quickly as possible, trying to get every one in the vicinity of the target. How far the ball goes does not matter. Nor does it matter how high or low you hit the ball. All that matters is that you make solid contact and hit the ball somewhere near your target line . . . and that you hit all six balls in twenty-five seconds or less.

By setting a time limit for hitting all six balls and by focusing solely on the target line (not distance, or flight, or trajectory), your brain will make subconscious adjustments to get your ball moving toward the intended target. Plus, your mind will not have time for all the invasive swing thoughts that tie you in knots. It worked for the caveman when he was out hunting for dinner with a spear and it was often a matter of life or death. He learned to throw the spear—a motion that is biomechanically similar to swinging a club at a ball—with precision and without thinking about it. My guess is, the caveman was unconcerned with head

Christopher hitting shots with six balls lined up in a row.

movement, body rotation, or weight shift as the saber-toothed tiger approached.

This is instinctive instead of analytical learning, so don't slow down, pause, or otherwise clutter your mind with thoughts. If you screw up all six shots, tee up six more balls and do it again. Just stick to your time limits: the less time you spend thinking about the golf swing and the more you react to a target, the quicker your mind and body will learn.

Next is a task I recommend whenever I have players who are having trouble hitting a particular club off line. More often than not, the club is the driver, and often they have begun to completely lose control of their golf ball. In those cases, I have students try and hit the driver 100 yards. That's right, 100 yards, with the intended ball flight. Once they can execute the 100-

yard drive, I move them up to 125, then 150, 175, 200, 225, and then finally near their normal driver distance. In scaling back, students can recapture the necessary feel and sensation that is often lost with high-energy swings. Interestingly enough, in "feeling" as though they are only going to hit the ball, say, 200 yards, more often than not the contact is such that the ball flies near their maximum distance, with much better control.

The brain is a mysterious organ. Its ability to adjust and adapt to get the body to perform the requested action far exceeds my or anyone else's ability to teach. Once you realize that and trust your abilities, you will be on your way to shooting lower scores.

"GOTTA KEEP MOVING ON"

Kids are phenomenal learners. Nonetheless, most juniors just love to whack golf balls without ever choosing a target . . . until the motorized range-ball picker rolls into view. Then, miraculously and quite unconsciously, their focus becomes highly refined. Since the ball picker is constantly on the move, there is no time to think about grip, posture, ball position, aim, alignment, backswing, weight shift, swing plane, lag, or releasing the club. The kids just see the picker, visualize a shot that will intercept it on its current course, and swing away. They see and react. In addition, depending on how far away the picker is, the kids must hit whatever club they have in their hands the appropriate distance, since there is no time to change clubs. I'm always astonished at the creativity and overall accuracy that is demonstrated when the picker shows up.

As childish as it might seem, you should try to hit the picker every once in a while. Not only will it improve your accuracy, you will find yourself making smoother and better golf swings without thinking about any paralyzing mechanics. You will improve your creativity and your instincts for hitting different shots, a critical component in improving your scores.

Perhaps no one in the history of golf has ever been such a magician with a golf ball as Seve Ballesteros— flop shots and greenside bunker shots to die for with a 1-iron, iron shots out of parking lots to win British

Christopher aiming for the ball picker.

Opens. Seve began to learn to control his golf ball as a kid whacking a 3-iron around on the beaches near his home in Santander, Spain. With that one club, he learned what made the ball go high, low, far, and near and curve in all directions. He did this out of passion, interest, and necessity, much the same as kids do when the ball picker comes into range.

WHAT YOU CAN LEARN FROM SPEED GOLF

Hauling fourteen clubs around the course for a round of speed golf would be like running a marathon with a backpack full of coal. I normally carry six clubs when I'm playing speed golf, although I've buzzed around with just a 5-iron in my hands to save time (not having to put the bag on the side of the green and pick it up again on the way to the next tee) and weight. The course isn't any shorter, but the time I have to play and the options I have in terms of club selection are, so I have to create shots on almost every hole. If a pin is tucked in the right corner of a green 160 yards away and my choices are 8-iron, which I hit a maximum of 150 yards, or 5-iron, which I normally hit 175ish, I have to create a shot with the clubs I have and make a split-second decision on which one has the highest chance of success. Do I close down the face of the 8-iron and hit a hard, low shot to get the extra ten yards, or do I grip down a couple of inches on the 5-iron and try to hit a soft cut, taking ten or fifteen yards off my normal shot? A lot of factors go into that decision, but I evaluate and make the call in a matter of seconds, always following my gut and using my "adaptive unconscious." In this example, I would more often than not opt for the "three-finger" 5-iron, as it provides more room for error.

The scores I shoot with six clubs are much better than the ones most people post with a full complement of fourteen clubs and a ball retriever. If you want to learn how to play for score instead of playing "golf swing" out on the course, try taking every other club out of your bag and playing a round with the ones that are left. You will find that being forced to create shots makes you think strategically. And it helps you learn the fundamental physics of the ball, the club, and the magic moment of impact, the most important nanosecond in golf.

SIX

O   O   O

"Get the Balance Right"

I had to dig deep in the CD closet to come up with a Depeche Mode title, but no song so far has been more accurate in its golf application.

There are no two ways about it: to hit a golf ball well, you have to "get the balance right." If you are not properly balanced—that is, not in control of your body throughout the swing—you will not hit a good shot. In fact, you stand a pretty good chance of whiffing it altogether. If you do make contact with a falling-down, catching-yourself, out-of-control swing, the results won't be pretty. No matter what kind of stroke you are playing, from the shortest putt to the longest drive, balance is absolutely critical to your success, because, as Arnold Palmer told his grandson, Sam Saunders, "If you're falling down after the shot, you most likely weren't in the right position during it."

No one demonstrates this point better than Tiger Woods. In addition to being one of the greatest athletes of his generation, Tiger might also be the most creative golfer who ever lived. No matter what precarious position he finds himself in, Tiger is always able to hit an unbelievable shot. Sometimes that means hitting a towering hook around a cluster of trees; other times it means pounding a screaming 200-yard cut shot that never gets above waist-high. Oftentimes the swings Tiger creates to hit those shots make him look like a top that is about to spin itself into the ground. But despite how these contorted motions appear, Tiger insists he always swings "within himself," which is another way of saying he is always in balance.

And he's right. Some of Tiger's swings look abbreviated, some look violent, and some look downright painful, but none of them, no matter how fast or how manufactured, look unbalanced. Tiger has the best body control of any golfer who ever played the game. From the standpoints of muscular control, coordination, strength, flexibility, and overall golf-swing-specific athleticism, he has no peer. As such, he can move the club in ways and at speeds most people cannot fathom. But to pull off these incredible shots, the greatest player in the game has to remain balanced throughout the swing, no matter what kind of swing that is. I'm convinced you could put Tiger on a unicycle and he could still hit a tee shot 290 yards.

I know he can hit the ball farther than most mortals while standing on one foot. That is part of his presentation during clinics. Tiger stands on his left foot and hits a driver that flies as straight as anything most golfers hit on their best days. He also hits balls with his right foot tucked behind his left during the backswing. Then he steps into the shot like a batter going after a fastball, and finishes standing on his left foot with his right in the air behind him.

These "trick shots" are not just for show: Tiger's point is that all kinds of shots can be created as long as you swing with control and balance. The alternative, as Tiger also shows in his clinic, is a swing where you fall backward so that you finish with your feet nowhere close to where they were at address. The result is a weak slice, an ugly ground ball, or a smother duck hook that can't get into the water hazard fast enough.

The only good golf shots you will ever hit are the ones where you remain balanced throughout your golf swing. And despite what you might think, that isn't as hard as it sounds.

"HOW LOOKS CAN BE DECEIVING"

To butcher a line from Elvis Costello, when it comes to balanced golf swings, "looks can be deceiving." Sure it's easy to see how smooth, classic swingers of the club like Ernie Els and Annika Sörenstam remain balanced throughout their motions. They are like ballet dancers, rhythmic and effortless as they pound shot after shot down the middle. But some of the funkiest golf swings in the world are also the most balanced.

You need look no farther than the King himself to see that this is true. Throughout his career, Arnold Palmer swung the club like a lumberjack going after a pine. His slashing, home-grown swing was part of his charm, a trait, along with hitching the front of his pants and winking at the crowds, that endeared him to the masses—"Look, Esther, he goes at it like me!"

But most fans failed to recognize the perfect balance Mr. Palmer exhibited throughout his golf swing. It might have looked like he was falling all over himself as he hung on to the club on the follow-through, but when analyzed in slow motion, it's obvious that Mr. Palmer's swing was a textbook example of balance trumping form every time. Despite how it looked, he never hit a good shot with an unbalanced golf swing.

On the opposite end of the spectrum, look at the photo on the next page of an average golfer making what he thinks is a smooth swing. Sure, the swing might not be as fast or swashbuckling as that of Arnold Palmer, but in truth I'd take Mr. Palmer's swing any day over this unbalanced motion. Or the swing may have the apparent speed of a Tour player's, but without the necessary muscular control and coordination (see chapter 9). The body cannot tolerate the excessive force, and overall stability is lost. If you swing the golf club with too much force, you will push yourself to the limits of your stability and lose control of your club, body, and the golf ball. The golf swing is not about how hard you can swing but about how much clubhead speed can you produce while maintaining stability and control.

We all need to find the maximum speed at which we can swing the club while maintaining reasonable coordination and balance. "You have to swing fast 'easy,'" my colleague and Top 100 teacher Jerry Mowlds always expounds. "Most people swing too hard—with too much effort and energy when trying to increase clubhead speed," he adds. The result is usually an unbalanced, out-of-control motion, one that screams of powerless effort as opposed to effortless power.

"Balance" is a term that is a bit misunderstood. The general public has melded "balance" and "stability" together as one. According to Donn Dimond, a physical therapist and clinic director in Beaverton, Oregon, for Physiotherapist Associates—the official health and fitness provider for all three major Tours (PGA, LPGA, and Champions)—"A loss of stability can lead to a loss of balance, which can lead to a fall. If your center of gravity goes outside your base of support and you do not have the ability to control it, you will lose your balance and fall."

So, from here on out, we will refer to any wobbly, whirling, and generally out-of-control motions as an issue of "stability" rather than "balance." Unless, of course, you are doing something where indeed you might find yourself on the ground.

An unstable swinging motion.

My stability is critical in speed golf as well, due to the fatigue factor. When I'm huffing and puffing by the back nine, it's easy for my tiring body to waver over the ball. If my stability is compromised before I swing, I'm off to a bad start. Perhaps nowhere is this more crucial than when putting: with an elevated heart rate in addition to overall body fatigue, I really have to focus on staying stable and quiet during the stroke.

"SCREAM IF YOU WANNA GO FASTER"

Even though this song reference conjures up long-forgotten images of the Spice Girls, I want you to rid your mind of music analogies for a second and think about race cars. If you've ever watched an auto race or taken any sort of passing interest in the sport, you know or have heard about the importance of fresh tires and having the proper spring and shock-absorber setup during a race. The reason for this is simple: for a race car to run fast, it must remain glued to the racetrack. For that to happen, the car must be balanced, which means that things like the air rushing over the spoiler, the pressure and camber of the tires, the strength of the springs, and the weight-to-thrust ratio must be aligned for maximum horsepower and grip. Only then can the car hold its momentum through the turns and run its fastest laps.

The same is true in golf. To generate maximum clubhead speed at the moment of impact, you have to be stable. If your stability is off-kilter, it will be like fighting an out-of-control race car: you will expend a lot of effort while generating very little speed. A finely balanced golf swing is one where the lower body (anchored, of course, by your feet) supports the unwinding torso and swinging arms so the club can release through impact (which is how a golfer generates the most controlled speed).

Christopher in a balanced finish position.

If all that happens, you will finish with your weight on your left side with your chest facing toward the target. But more important, you will be completely balanced, not falling over or quickstepping to catch yourself. The clubhead will also move faster through impact, leading to longer, more accurate shots.

"GET SOME BALANCE LIKE A BIKE WITHOUT THE KICKSTAND"

"So, Christopher, how do you build balance into your golf game?" you ask. "Isn't it like foot speed? You're either born a track star or you are not, and no amount of training will make you run a ten-flat hundred meters if your natural speed is closer to a twelve. Aren't balance and clubhead speed like that?"

I don't mean to waffle, but the answer is both yes and no. Yes, you have some natural, hereditary limitations on how much clubhead speed you will be able to generate. Good genes, proto-plasm, and fast twitch-muscle fibers are a few of the elements that can help a golfer swing the club at high speeds and still stay vertical. Unless you are a gifted athlete with quick hands and a lot of natural, God-given talent—or you have decided to basically live in the gym and trade your wife and kids for a personal trainer and perhaps some HGH (human growth hormone) to be named later—you won't be able to generate 130-mile-per-hour clubhead speed. But by improving your stability and technique you will be able to generate a lot more clubhead speed than you do right now. And with a clubhead speed of only 105 miles an hour (a very attainable goal), you can fly a tee shot 250 yards. Wouldn't that be nice?

On the same front, balance is made of three systems: the eyes, the inner ear, and the muscles and nerves working together. All of the information from these senses goes straight to the brain for processing. The better these three systems work individually and together, the better stability and balance you will have.

If you have problems in those areas (vertigo, for example), there isn't a lot you can do in golf to improve that condition. But if you are like most people, a little klutzy on the dance floor and a tad light-headed when you jump up off the couch but otherwise fine, then you can improve both your balance and, by extension, your clubhead speed through practice.

"The more you train your balance/stability system, the more force it can handle and the more clubhead speed you can control," adds Dimond. "The best way to train is to make sure you are training each system—the eyes, inner ears, and muscles. A good beginning exercise is standing on one foot for at least thirty seconds without falling over. Once you can do this, then repeat, but try moving your opposite arm across your chest for fifteen repetitions. After you master this, try standing on one leg while you close your eyes, and then try standing on one leg, closing your eyes, and reaching across your body."

There are plenty of golf-specific games to get you there as well. Some of the most universal include:

"COME TOGETHER"

With a short club (a wedge or a 9-iron to start), hit balls with your feet together. You will have to start by making a shorter swing than normal—maybe half or three-quarters—to keep from falling down. But once you get the feel for swinging this way, you will probably find that you're making solid contact more consistently than you were with a wide stance.

Once you get comfortable with this game, you will also be surprised how far you hit the ball. Keeping your feet together stops you from throwing the club at the ball from the top of the backswing, overswinging, using excessive lower body and leg movement, and dipping and lunging at the ball—shot killers one and all. A narrow stance forces you to generate speed at the bottom of the swing (where both the ball and your feet are).

The great Ernest Jones, renowned instructor and author of *Swing the Clubhead*, played his best golf after losing his right leg below the knee during combat in World War I. He thereafter balanced himself on one leg and at a mere five feet five inches and 130 pounds would routinely shoot around par. Casey Martin, former Nationwide Tour winner and U.S. Open participant (he tied for twenty-third in the 1998 championship) and one of the better ball strikers in all of golf today, makes his full swing basically swinging on one leg (his left) due to the Klippel-Trenaunay-Weber syndrome (KTW) in his right leg. Makes you wonder about the importance of a weight shift, doesn't it?

After hitting lots of balls from this stance, work your way up to longer clubs, and then slowly work yourself back into a normal stance, first separating your feet by no more than a couple of inches, then gradually moving them farther and farther apart until you are making the same solid swing from a normal stance.

If at any point in this drill you revert back to your old habits or bad shot patterns, go back to the beginning with your feet together and start again. Not only does going back to the beginning each time you hit a bad shot add incentive and improve your concentration, it also keeps you from rushing this game before the benefits are fully realized.

"STEP BY STEP"

Eddie Rabbitt is an avid golfer who has a good little swing. But he wasn't thinking about his game when he wrote "Step by Step." That hasn't stopped me from using it as an example

Christopher getting ready to swing with feet together.

of what you can do to improve your balance and consistency.

Take your normal stance, and then lift your left foot and place it behind your right with your left heel in the air. All your weight will be on your right foot, with your left toe touching the ground somewhere behind you.

Now swing the club back, then step into the shot, moving your left foot back to its original position as the backswing ends or the forward swing begins. If you are unstable, you will hit the ground well behind the ball. You might also hit the dreaded shank a few times before you get the feel of it. Neither of these is good, but both are to be expected, and the point of this exercise is primarily to help capture the proper feel in the backswing, so if need be, don't even swing down. Most people overcomplicate the golf swing within the first few inches of the

LEFT: Christopher with his left heel next to his right toe.
RIGHT: Christopher just before impact, having stepped into the shot.

takeaway by adding unnecessary motions. By swinging with your feet in this fashion, you will be forced to simplify the takeaway or loose your stability.

Don't think you will look foolish working on this drill. Vijay Singh still does it all the time to get the club in the right position at the top. If it's good enough for Vijay, you shouldn't have a problem with it.

"YOUR HEELS SO HIGH"

A lot of very smart people have passionate opinions on whether the lower body initiates the downswing, or whether the arms lead and the lower body follows. Some great teachers have wasted a lot of brain matter arguing both sides of this point. I couldn't care less, nor do I think you can tell people what to feel in their golf swings any more than you can dictate what kind of music they have to like.

Unquestionably, as in all throwing and hitting motions, there is a lateral move of the lower body, and the hips rotate toward the target as a player's weight shifts, so that he is standing on his left foot after impact. How you get there is totally up to you. But if you clutter your mind with "shift your weight!" thoughts during the swing, the results won't be pretty. Ted Williams didn't think about how to hit a pitch, Muhammad Ali

Close-up of Christopher's foot at address with a golf ball underneath his right heel.

didn't think about how to throw a punch, and you don't have to think about how to make a golf ball go forward.

To get yourself in position to move your legs, hips, and arms through impact in a stable fashion, try putting a golf ball underneath your right heel at address. This will force you to cut out any unnecessary sliding or shifting you might have worked into your backswing. It will also give you a head start on getting onto your left side coming forward, something a lot of players struggle with and a flaw that causes you to lose gobs of club-head speed.

Again, don't feel foolish working on this drill. It is a favorite of Tour players like Charles Howell III, who is, pound for pound, one of the longest hitters in golf.

"I'M GONNA HOLD, HOLD ON"

It's hard to believe, but I can't tell you the number of people I have taught who stumble around the tee like a bus-station drunk during their swings but have no idea that they have stability problems. Once the swing is over and they have caught themselves before falling face-first off the lesson tee, they seem to think everything was fine.

I always give those people a very simple game to prove my point: take your normal stance and swing but hold your finish until the ball hits the ground, then tap your back foot three times. Don't recoil or fall back and reset. Finish the swing and hold it just until the ball comes down, then tap away.

Not only will you find this task to be more difficult than you imagined, you will see pretty quickly how unstable you are during and after your golf swing.

Christopher hitting balls barefooted.

"DANCING BAREFOOT"

A great summertime game is to hit drivers barefoot and see how long it takes you to hit the ball farther than you normally do fully shod. If you are like most people, you will slip and slide all over the turf for the first few swings. Then, as the brain learns and adjusts from your past less-than-perfect shots, you will start hitting long, solid drives that fly straighter and farther than you could ever have imagined possible.

This game was a favorite of Sam Snead's and has always been a staple for the longer hitters. John Daly works on it quite a bit, as does Laura Davies, one of the longest hitters in the history of women's golf.

For those who think these games are too difficult or who don't see the point in all this stability stuff, consider the fact that Jason Zuback, a four-time Long Drive Champion, can actually hit a tee shot over 300 yards while standing on one of those large physioballs, the kind you see in gyms for crunches and core and back exercises.

Christopher making swings on a half foam roller.

"I started out trying to kneel on the ball, just to work on my balance," Zuback says. "Once I got up there, I figured I'd try to stand. That took a while, but once I got up, I started swinging a club. Then I realized I could actually hit the ball from up there, and make a better swing than I was making with both feet on the ground."

Annika Sörenstam can do the same thing (although she isn't as long as Zuback), an impressive feat and an example of the importance placed on balance by the best players in the world.

If the physioball is a bit extreme, start on a half foam roller or pillowlike discs. It's not necessary at first to hit a ball; just make a few swings on the roller or discs, then back on the ground. On the aforementioned objects, your stability will be challenged and the ground will become a welcome—and stable—relief.

WHAT YOU CAN LEARN FROM SPEED GOLF

Sprinting between shots take its toll on the body, none bigger than the balance issues speed golfers experience late in the round. Like all runners, speed golfers have a lot of oxygen churning through their lungs as they sprint from tee to green. That oxygenation leaves us feeling light-headed at times, just as a champion marathon runner might seem a bit wobbly as he crosses the finish line. The more oxygen you have in your lungs, the more is in your bloodstream, which means more is getting to your brain, causing you to feel a little dizzy.

Because of that inherent dizziness, I have to pay close attention to my balance throughout a round of speed golf, often taking one extra club and making half- or three-quarter swings when I start to feel a little light-headed, just to make sure I hit the ball solid on the clubface and keep it moving in the right direction.

I also focus on my tempo, making sure I find and keep a constant swing pace even though I'm running between shots. There is no time for practice swings in speed golf, and to reiterate, during a round of golf—whether you're running, walking, or riding between shots—it's too late to practice. As I arrive at my ball, I pick the club, gather myself physically and mentally, and make as balanced and fluid a swing as possible.

○ ○ ○

SEVEN

"You Save Me"

Kenny Chesney's lyrics sum it up: "Baby you save me."

Okay, Kenny wasn't singing about an errant tee shot ending up behind a tree, or a squib approach shot plugging under the lip of a bunker. But every golfer can relate to the feelings Kenny describes in this touching ballad. You hit a screwball into a squirrelly lie and think, "I'm cooked now," only to hit a miraculous recovery to salvage par. Love would not be too strong a word for the feeling this kind of save elicits.

Unfortunately, those miraculous recoveries don't happen very often. The more likely scenario goes like this: you push your approach shot on a par four way right, and the ball hits the cart path before coming to rest near a tree. From there you try a high wedge shot, but you hit so far behind the ball that a pinecone flies farther. Then you chunk another one, getting dirt on your trousers and leaving the ball short of a greenside bunker. Determined not to hit another one fat, you take a good cut at the next shot, hitting a screaming, ankle-high skull across the green where your partners high-step out of the way as the ball shoots into a water hazard. That's when you put the wedge away and say, "I'm done."

Certainly you recognize that story. I know you've been there. You are probably guilty of the aftermath sin as well: the one where you go to the next hole blaming the pushed approach shot for the big black X on your scorecard. Never mind that you were sitting just to the right of the green after your second shot. With a reasonable pitch somewhere on the green, you would have had a putt for par. If you are a decent putter, the worst you would have walked away with was bogey, and, if you hit a great pitch and/or putt, you might have made the same score as the fellow who hit a perfect approach to the center of the green and two-putted. But you walk to the next hole grumbling that the pushed iron shot ruined your whole round. All those chunks, flubs, and low, skulled screamers with the wedge are forgotten.

This attitude leads to more bad scores than anything else in golf. And a bad attitude in golf causes more damage than a bad swing.

More than any other question, I am most often asked, "Christopher, I don't want to be great, but what can I do to stop shooting these high numbers and become at least a halfway decent golfer?"

My answer is simple. I tell any of those high handicappers who will listen that "I can knock a minimum of ten shots off your score within a year with one simple lesson." That statement gets a lot of attention, until I deliver the punch line. "You need to devote five hours a week to practicing—much of which you can do at home—but, for at least a year, you can never hit a practice shot that is longer than a hundred yards."

Whether it's the five-hours-a-week commitment or the prohibition on ripping drives down the range that gets them, I usually lose most people after that statement. But there's more. I also say, "If you practice only short shots, recovery shots, or as my late, great friend and mentor Paul Runyan called them, 'partial shots,' for a year, hitting nothing but wedges and putters, you will lower your average score by five to ten strokes or more, depending on your present handicap."

Nota bene: I don't guarantee anything in this game!

Strangely, the thought of shooting lower scores doesn't seem to always arouse a lot of interest. Most people consider practicing their pitches, chips, and bunker shots to be "boring" or "not really practice," or "not what I need to work on," which is the biggest lie of all. They choose to go on trying to build the perfect full swing, working on hitting their tee shots farther and wasting precious time cluelessly practicing on the putting green.

Average players could improve faster and shave more shots off their scores if they practiced nothing but partial shots. Unfortunately, most of them won't. I have seen players who practice three and four times a week, who hit ball after ball on the range, who never look twice at the short-game area and practice-putting green. If they do practice a fifty- or sixty-yard shot, it is as a warm-up for the full swings, a few wedges here and there to get the muscles warm before pulling out the driver and flailing away.

It would be easy to write off this quirk as just some manly need to hit the ball long and hard. If the short-game area is used by anyone, it is better players, the very people who, you would think, would be most susceptible to testosterone-driven urges.

For years I tried to figure out why so many people who so desperately needed to practice partial wedge shots treated the short-game area like a leper colony. I asked my students why they spent so little time practicing the shots that could save them the most strokes during a round. Most gave the standard "I don't have time" or "I really need to work on my drives" excuses, which I didn't buy. The bottom line is, higher handicappers don't practice the short shots because they don't know how and what to practice and, yes, there is not as much overall enjoyment or satisfaction compared with a perfectly struck full shot. However, we all like to look at the scorecard after eighteen holes and see the lowest score possible, and on and around the green is where it is all starts.

"AAH RECOVERY"

The beautiful chorus by that name comes from a band called Kosheen, whose singer, Sian Evans, again, would be stunned to learn that I am using her words in a golf lesson. But the importance of partial, recovery shots cannot be overstated, so I want to beat the drum and tell everyone within shouting distance that they should "feel happy when they're living it," because the joy that comes with getting up and down for par makes you want to sing and dance, or at least whistle as you head to the next tee.

It should surprise no one that Tiger Woods leads the Tour in the number of greens he hits in regulation. But even the best in the world never hits every green. Tiger hits 73 percent of the greens in regulation. That means he misses the green 27 percent of the time—that's one out of four greens on any given day that Tiger Woods, the best player in the world, misses.

To assume you are not going to miss any greens is pure folly. Going back to the Tiger Woods example, when he first came out on tour, one of the knocks on his game was his wedge game and its relative lack of variety. Lots of high, spinning shots with fuller shots—and not much else. Now Tiger is near the top on the Tour in sand saves and recoveries while leading in greens hit in regulation; the plethora of half- and three-quarter wedge shots he now possesses is something to behold. He accomplished this amazing feat by deciding that he was going to become the best wedge player ever. With Butch Harmon, he worked tirelessly on improving his ability to get up and down from anywhere, and he has continued the pattern with Hank Haney. Want to put your money on someone to get it up and down from just about anywhere? As with most things in golf, put your dough on TW. That work has obviously paid off for him, just as it will for you.

No one this side of Tiger is going to hit 75 percent of the greens they play in regulation. An average handicapper will be lucky to hit five or six greens a round. A high handicapper would be thrilled to hit two or three. If you hit half your greens in regulation, you are among the best amateur players in your state, and if you hit two-thirds and can putt at all you are probably one of the best amateurs in the country.

That means you hit recovery or partial shots on half or more of the holes you play. And yet, if you are in the majority, these are the shots you practice the least.

My friend and coauthor, Steve Eubanks, learned this lesson the hard way. In August of 2006, Steve underwent heart surgery in which he had a pacemaker and defibrillator installed. Due to the wires running into the chambers of his heart, the surgeon told Steve he could not swing a golf club for six to eight weeks. "You can chip and putt, but anything more and you risk pulling the wires loose from the lower ventricles," he said, which I assume is a very bad thing. For eight weeks, Steve did nothing but work on his short game, chipping, putting, hitting sand shots, throwing a dozen balls around a green in varying lies and seeing if he could get them all up and down, that sort of thing.

Eight weeks to the day after his surgery, the doctor gave Steve the go-ahead and he jumped onto the first tee. In his first round of golf in two months, having not taken a full swing since his surgery, Steve shot 69 with six birdies. Now, he's a pretty good player, having played in college. But that was one of his best rounds of the year, not because he hit the ball better than he ever had, but because he got up and down from everywhere and hit it close to the hole every time he had a wedge in his hands.

Heart surgery is an extreme way to learn any lesson, but this is a great example of the impact practicing your partial shots can have on your game.

"WHY'S IT SO HARD?"

Another reason that partial shots get so little attention is the maddening number of things most people do to complicate these short shots. Let's face it, you could pick up the ball and throw it closer than you hit most of your chips and pitches and bunker shots. Still, these short shots fill the mind with all kinds of gremlins. The most prominent include:

- Keep the left wrist firm.

- Cock the wrists quickly.

- Keep the clubface square throughout the stroke.

- Open the clubface quickly and slide it underneath the ball.

- Narrow your stance, open your feet, hips, and shoulders to the target line, and put more weight on your left side.

- Take your normal stance.

- Pull the club down with the left arm.

- Pitch the club with the right arm like throwing a softball underhanded.

- Keep your sternum over the ball and hit down and through the short shots with no wrist action.

- Make sure your head is steady and get the club up quickly.

- Release the club quickly, turning the left palm up right after impact.

- Hold on to the club through impact, keeping the clubface turned skyward throughout the stroke.

- Make the stroke long and slow.

- Shorter and faster through impact, imparting a lot of spin is better.

- Stand taller over short shots.

- Grip down on the club and bend over more for better control.

- Hit two inches behind the ball in a bunker with your normal swing.

- Take a longer-than-normal swing and hit six inches behind the ball in the bunker.

- Hit closer to the ball for longer bunker shots and farther away for shorter shots.

- Open the clubface and the stance in the bunker.

- Keep the clubface and stance square in the bunker.

It's no wonder most people avoid the short-game area. It's frustrating for shots that short to be so complicated. Even the terminology is confusing to many. Chips, pitches, bumps, lobs, etc. Why must we give everything a name and title? It's a less than full swing, period—and enough said. Yes, sometimes we want the ball to fly high and roll a little; sometimes we want the ball to fly low and roll a lot. It's basically the club that changes the height and roll, or some use the same club and control the ball the same way as when we toss a ball different distances and trajectories. So I can appreciate the apprehension you have as I tell you to take a shag bag to the short-game area and spend the afternoon hitting short ones. If my mind were cluttered with all those conflicting thoughts, I would have reservations about pulling the wedge out too.

But you don't have to think about all those things to hit great short shots. In fact, the best way to learn to get up and down is to forget all those crazy how-tos, free your mind of all the garbage, and trust your body to learn through trial and error—and once again, a lot of it. Given the fact that no two short shots are the same, that is really the only way to learn to get the ball up and down. The likelihood of practicing every conceivable partial shot and perfecting it to the point where you can pull it off without any problem during a round is laughably small. Yet that is apparently what the great short-game performers do—the Tigers, Olazábals, and Ballesteroses, day in and day out. How so? Time, creativity, and perseverance.

I go back to the example of Seve Ballesteros. One of the first times I saw Seve, he was playing at Riviera Country Club in the L.A. Open and had what I thought was an unplayable lie under a bush. Not only was the ball nestled inches below the low-hanging shrub, there was a sand trap between Seve's ball and the hole, with the pin tucked only a few feet onto the green. Most mortals would have taken an unplayable, dropped, and then struggled to make double bogey. So imagine my surprise when Seve took out a 1-iron, got down on his knees, and hit a punch shot that never got off the ground but ran through the bunker and onto the green five feet from the pin. After he made the putt for par, I heard another member of the gallery say, "Wonder how many times he practiced that shot?"

The answer is, probably many times. Rather than plopping down a pile of balls and hitting them all from the same place to the same hole with the same club from a perfect lie, Seve, like all great partial-shot masters, has practiced and hit such a myriad and quantity of different shots, it would boggle one's mind. Seve had hit enough recovery shots in his life and had created more shots than most people could imagine, so he had full confidence in trying to roll a 1-iron through a bunker from under a bush. In addition, when you grow up with a cut-down 3-iron as your only club, as Seve did, your imagination is jump-started, and you learn to make the ball do things that most mortals can't do with multiple wedges. Speaking of multiple wedges, I am of the belief that most people (low handicappers excluded) who play with three or four wedges aren't very good with any one of them. If you belong to that group, ditch all but one wedge for a while and learn to hit different shots with one club. Now, you may never reach the level of creativity that Seve did with his 3-iron, but you can improve your vision, technique, imagination, and execution around the greens with a few simple games.

THROW SOME BALLS

Using the "five-finger" wedge is a great way to help you picture short shots. You can do this from a variety of spots and distances around the green. Stand as you normally would for a partial shot—slightly facing the target, or "open"—and toss the ball so it finishes near the hole. The goal is to fill your head with images of the trajectory and roll necessary to get the ball close to, or in, the hole. Take note how your entire body feels and reacts, particularly your right hand and the different way it releases the ball depending on the height and speed required.

Now, as you are doing this, are you thinking about how much to rotate your shoulders going back? What your head is doing during the tossing motion? Where your weight is? Keeping your wrist in front of your fingers? I think not. Partial shots are basically a matter of making a mini motion picture in your head of what you are trying to do with the ball, bringing the feel of that picture into the body—especially the dominant hand—then doing it without any conscious interference. See it, do it. If you have learned how to toss, you can learn to hit the short shots.

"STAY ON YOUR TOES"

The song "Stay on Your Toes" is by Del tha Funkee Homosapien, a classic I'm sure you have on your playlist. The title does serve as a wonderfully accurate description of the first game you should play to become more proficient with short recovery shots. This is a "bulk practice" game, focusing on technique, to help you learn to strike your partial shots more cleanly, crisply, and solidly.

With a wedge, I want you to throw down ten balls a few yards from the chipping green. Now pick a target and try to hit all ten as close as possible while standing with your left foot firmly planted but your right heel elevated so that you are on the tiptoes of your right foot—standing a bit like a flamingo. This is going to be difficult for a few swings, as you are probably accustomed to shifting and sliding your weight around during even the shortest of strokes, and most of your weight is now on your left leg and foot. Balance could be a problem. But once you get the hang of it, you will find that you are making a lot better contact with a much shorter, more compact swing, exactly the swing you need to use when hitting small shots.

Once you are comfortable hitting the shot you've chosen on your right tiptoes, change the shot a bit—hit a few from a longer distance and a few from a spot a little closer to the hole. Try hitting some low runners and a few high pitches, all with the same club and the same stance. I want you to feel a compact, small swing with minimal lower-body action, and I want to see how quickly you can learn to repeat that stroke and adapt it to different situations.

"TWIST MY ARM"

Just as you did when you worked on the grip, to get an accurate feel for how to hit different short shots, grip your wedge with only your left hand, and hit several shots onto the chipping green. Once you learn to make solid contact with your right arm behind your back (again, something that isn't going to happen immediately), you will find that the ball jumps off the clubface a little lower than normal and the ball rolls out quite a long way on the green. This is important information for when you have a short area to carry but a lot of green between your ball and the hole. The stroke you practice with your left arm only is the feel you will ultimately have when you are hitting this low running pitch shot.

After you get comfortable hitting this shot to one target, throw a few balls around the fringe and pick some different spots on the green to try to hit. Knowing how far the ball flies and rolls with one hand is very important. And your brain will remember. Once you hit a shot, it is stored in your memory banks forever to be recalled on the golf course when the situation arises, as long as you don't let your conscious mind get in the way.

Now put your left arm behind your back and hit balls with only your right. The first thing you are going to notice is how much higher you hit the ball and how much longer your swing has to be to hit it the same distance you are hitting it with your left arm. This is what a flop shot feels like. It is also the feeling you need to log into your memory bank for that moment on the course when you need a high, soft shot that flies a short distance and stops quickly.

In general, right-handed players would do well to feel that most partial shots are played primarily with the dominant hand. As noted above, a firmer left hand will tend to make the ball come out lower and hence roll more, but in general you righties don't have much coordination or control with the left side of your bodies. So let the right hand and arm take over, once again, much as if you were tossing a ball. Tiger himself feels as if he hits his short shots from around the green primarily with his right (his dominant) hand.

Christopher hitting shots with right hand/arm only, while talking on his cell phone.

Once you get a handle on the right-hand shot, mix it up as well, picking a few different targets and scattering your practice balls around the fringe so that you have different looks and different lies. If you hit one shot bad, try another shot or two from the same spot, then move to a different location and finish hitting all your balls. You aren't getting any floating mulligans on the course; there's no reason to take any on the chipping green.

CELL-PHONE PHENOMENON

The omnipresence of the cell phone has created a fascinating phenomenon around the green. I often see people practicing their short shots while talking on the phone—and with strikingly positive results: phone in the left ear being held by the left hand, club in the right hand. Swinging away with perfect tempo, contact and distance control remarkably good. Once the conversation is over, the phone goes in the pocket, the left hand back on the club, and often the results go downhill. Why?

A couple of reasons: first off, with only the right hand on the club (most people's dominant hand), the motion is more intuitive and natural, very much like tossing something underhand. We humans normally toss with one hand, not two. Secondly, when we are talking, the conscious part of the mind is occupied and therefore unable to offer disturbing thoughts on "how to" swing the club or move the body. For individuals with chronic short-game issues (and yippers), hitting these shots with only the dominant hand is frequently a good solution.

THE LINE GAME

This game is one of Nick Faldo's favorites. Tee up a ball or place a medium-size object (a hula hoop works well) at the edge of the practice green. Take twenty golf balls, placing the first one only a yard away from your target, the next another yard farther back, and so on. Grab your favorite wedge (only one) and, starting with the closest ball, try to hit the target object on the fly while working your way back. The goal is to land your ball on the target object—nothing else. No mechanical/technique-oriented thoughts. Do this in a relatively rapid but unhurried fashion. When you are finished, lay down another twenty balls and work forward from the one that is farthest from the target.

Once you've mastered this with your favorite wedge, try some different clubs—9-iron, 6-iron, another wedge, whatever. Hit some shots out of different lies, and once you've become proficient with several clubs, extend your line to thirty to fifty yards. Then experiment with hitting balls higher and lower with the same club. The feedback from the game is extremely valuable, since each shot is only slightly different in distance from the previous one. Watch how different clubs make the ball roll different ways and for different distances, and begin to get an instinctual feel for distance and the importance of good contact.

"SWARMING LIKE A DOZEN CRUSHING BLOWS"

Bassist Mike Mills from R.E.M., the band that authored those lyrics, is not only a golfer; he's an avid player with a single-digit handicap. But the song has nothing to do with golf, even though the lyrics are a perfect setup for the next game.

I want you to hold a dozen balls in your hands and march ten paces away from the chipping green. Then I want you to throw the balls straight up in the air. You might have to duck and cover to keep from being hit in the head, but that's okay. Now, wherever the balls come down is where they lie. From there, try to get all twelve up and down to the same hole on the green. Have your

putter ready, and count how many balls you down in two. Once you reach a point where you can get ten out of twelve up and down from the random lies you draw when throwing the balls in the air, you're ready for prime time.

"MY BEST SIDE WAS YOUR WORST"

Even the small minority of golfers who do practice their short recovery shots usually do so badly. They waste a lot of time and energy hitting shots they will never see on the golf course.

Christopher throwing a dozen balls in the air, to be played from where they land.

For example, when you miss a green on the golf course, the ball usually rolls into the rough, or onto a sidehill lie, or in a bunker, or next to a cart path, or on pine straw near the shrubbery, or in a collection area near a sprinkler head, or . . . you get the point. Rarely does the ball come to rest perched perfectly on a tuft of grass with an open line to the flag. Yet that is exactly the shot most people practice when they do venture into the short-game area. Almost never do I see someone throwing a ball into the gnarly rough on the side of a hill so that one foot is in the bunker and the other is above the ball, even though that lie is a lot more common on the golf course than the perfect lie just in front of the hole.

Christopher practicing a shot out of long grass.

In order for your short-game practice to have meaning, you should simulate the most outrageous shots you can imagine, working on the worst lies, the deepest rough, the most extreme stances from uphill, downhill, and sidehill lies. Throw three balls as hard as you can into the deepest rough you can find, and see how many of them you can get up and down (or even on the green). Then find a severe downhill slope, and try to pitch the ball to an elevated green. Then toss six balls on the pine straw near the azaleas, and see how close you get them to the flag.

This is how the greatest short-game players in the world learned their craft. Ben Crenshaw and Tom Kite used to play games like H-O-R-S-E around the chipping green by picking outrageous shots and seeing who could get the ball up and down. "Flop shot over the bunker from the rough in a downhill, sidehill lie for an R, Tom."

"You're on, Ben."

Tiger spends hours creating the most challenging shots he can find, then working on them until he can get the ball close to the hole every time. It is that creativity and work ethic that has made him one of the best short-game players who ever lived.

"GET YOUR FINGER OFF THE TRIGGER"

This lyric is from an Anouk song called "In the Sand." And the "get your finger off the trigger" line applies to a lot of the people I see thrashing around in the bunkers. Some of them become so despondent at their inability to get out of bunkers that I want to say, "Put down all sharp objects and step slowly away from the ledge."

For years I've heard a lot of golf pros spout some line about the sand shot being one of the easiest shots in golf because you don't actually have to hit the ball, just the sand somewhere around it. Hearing this sort of nonsense only adds to the frustration most amateurs feel after they've tossed more sand than a Saudi grave digger without coming close to getting their golf balls out. Sand shots are hard for the same reason high, soft pitch shots are a bear: you haven't practiced them enough to know what works for you and what doesn't. Plus, let's be honest: you're basically standing in a hole filled with ground rock, attempting to make the ball float out like a helium balloon and land as soft as a baby's bottom. Throw in the fact that banging around in a sand trap is the psychological equivalent of a Singapore caning, and it's easy to see why so many people have anxiety attacks when it comes to learning sand shots.

The great Claude Harmon, winner of the 1948 Masters (as a club pro), was one of the best bunker players ever. He insisted on only a few things in the bunker, and one of them was the need to hit the sand. "There are five tons of sand in the average greenside bunker; you've got to hit some of it!" Claude would expound.

Indeed, hitting some sand—with enough swing to move the sand out of the bunker—is one of the few "musts" in a greenside bunker. Another critical element to successful sand play is consistently hitting the same spot in the sand slightly behind the ball. This is where most of my students struggle the most. One time the club will enter the sand two or three inches behind the ball, the next six or eight inches behind. That one is often followed by a swing where not one grain of the five tons present is displaced and the ball sails over the green (or into the lip) like a Scud missle.

To remedy this predicament and learn to consistently hit the same spot in the sand, it can be highly beneficial to get rid of the ball. Since we are standing in a large crevasse, attempting to launch a ball high in the air out of it, our instincts lead us to try to lift or pick the ball out of the greenside bunker. This is a contradictory feeling from that of hitting a spot a couple of inches behind the ball.

Draw a line in the sand from one edge of the bunker to the other. Start at one end of the line and simply try to hit the line with your club, with enough swing that the sand exits the bunker. Work your way down the line, adjusting as need be to hit that line while trying to take the same depth of sand while you're at it. Once you can do this with some precision, plop a ball down in the bunker, draw a little line a couple of inches behind it, and focus on bringing the club down on the line. If you are somewhere in the vicinity of the line, the ball comes out. If you find, like many players, that once you have reintroduced the ball into the equation, your line-striking proficiency becomes erratic, go back to "walking the line." Eventually you will be less concerned with the ball itself and more focused on the task of hitting the spot/line in the sand slightly behind the ball.

I believe that before you can become an effective sand player, you have to overcome your fear of being in the bunker. The only way to do that is to make it fun. For starters, I want you to take a couple of balls into the practice bunker, but rather than throwing them down into the sand, build a small cone, a sand castle of sorts, just as you would on the beach. Then place a ball on top of the cone as if it were an oversize tee, and see how easy it is to hit the ball out of the bunker from there.

Repeat that process numerous times—build moats around your castles, and maybe draw a door and a window or two in them, before destroying them by hitting a ball off the top. You will be stunned how quickly your fear of the sand will evaporate as you play this little game with yourself. And you'll be equally surprised by how well you hit the ball off your makeshift tee.

If you think this game is only for toddlers in the backyard sandbox, think again. Butch Harmon tells a story about how Seve wanted to bet him a few years ago that he could hit a ball out of a greenside bunker with both ends of a rake. He briefly pondered the bet before remembering just how brilliant the Spaniard is out of the sand. Remember, Seve hit most of those shots as a kid with the cut-down 3-iron on the beach near his home in Santander, Spain. Butch didn't take the bet, but he did ask to see the feat. So Seve calmly put a ball in the sand and flipped the head end of the rake so it looked like a funky croquet-style mallet, gripped down a bit, and splashed the ball and a little sand out of the bunker. He then proceeded to build a mound of sand in the bunker, placed the ball on top of it, got down on his knees, and whacked the tip of the mound just under the ball with the butt end of the rake, making the ball fly out. Money well saved for Butch. Wonder if his dad knew that one.

The other obstacle many people must overcome in the sand is their inability to focus on a target. Most high-handicap players forget where the hole, or even the green, is when they get in the sand. The only thing they focus on is getting out, or more aptly, "Don't leave it in the bunker!"—which is exactly what they do. By forgetting about the target, these players become ball bound and focused on a negative instead of a positive.

Christopher hitting a sand shot off a built-up cone in the sand.

To overcome that mental block, I recommend that players practice hitting sand shots away from the green. Pick a spot out in the fairway or in the chipping area next to the bunker—find a pinecone or a rock or some other object you can focus on as a target—and hit toward that. By taking away your normal visual cues, the green, the hole, and the flag, your brain will automatically focus on the new and interesting target.

Another question I'm asked all the time is, "Christopher, how much sand should I take when I'm hitting out of a bunker?" or "How far behind the ball should I try to hit?" Neither of those questions can be answered, because I have no idea how far you are trying to hit the ball. There are indeed many ways to control the distance out of a greenside bunker, and amount of sand and how far behind the ball to hit are certainly two of those ways. However, I believe that the simpler the motion and

Christopher hitting sand shots away from the green.

task, the easier it is to learn, execute, and repeat.

Rather than trying to take different depths of sand (this is golf, not geology) or mastering hitting one-half, three, and six inches behind the ball, try making different-length swings to make the ball go different distances, all while hitting the same spot in the sand behind the ball and taking the same swath of sand. If you had to throw or toss the ball out of the bunker, how would you do it? Well, for a short bunker shot, your arm would move more slowly and less; and for a longer one, your arm would swing faster and more—all unconsciously.

A good way to learn this feel—and be able to check yourself—is to change the length of your follow-through to fit the length of the shot to play. So, for a shortish bunker shot, aim for your spot a couple inches behind the ball and finish with a short follow-through; medium-length bunker shot—medium follow-through/finish; long bunker shot—long follow-through/finish. In "holding" your finish position, you can monitor what has happened during the swing and begin to capture the sensations of different swing lengths and speeds to hit the ball different distances.

"THE ANSWER IS IN FRONT OF YOU"

Recovery and short shots are called "scoring shots" for a reason. They are the shots that can make or break your score in any

Christopher swinging in a bunker and holding the finish.

round. Not only does your ability to hit these chips, pitches, and sand shots improve the likelihood that you will have more pars on the card, your long game will improve as well. Your confidence in your own ability to get the ball up and down eliminates a lot of the pressure you put on yourself to hit the green and avoid bunkers. When you know you don't have to hit it close, because you are proficient from around the green, you'll end up making freer and better golf swings on all your approach shots.

WHAT YOU CAN LEARN FROM SPEED GOLF

In a round of speed golf, I have neither the time nor the inclination to ponder which club to use on any particular partial shot. Plus, my options are much more limited than yours, since I only play with six clubs. Chipping with a 3-wood or a hybrid looks cool on Sundays when a Tour player does it, but I don't have time to even think about such things, so I go with my gut and instinct—which always leads me to the club in which I have the most confidence. I hit most of my short shots with my 53-degree wedge (my only wedge when playing speed golf). And when it comes to hitting recovery shots, like most other shots in golf, confidence is well over half the battle.

My bunker play has improved tremendously since I've begun to play and practice with only the 53-degree wedge. Give me something with more loft now and it seems like cheating. If you are already a reasonably good bunker player, make your practice harder if you want to continue to progress. Hit some bunker shots with a 9-iron, then a 7-iron, and eventually a 5-iron. Experiment with different setups and swings to see how you can make a midlofted iron act like a sand wedge. When you think you're pretty good with the 5-iron in just getting it out, consider that José María Olazábal can hit the same greenside bunker shots with his 1-iron that he can with his sand wedge.

Conversely, if you are like many amateurs, newer players, or higher handicappers, you probably don't practice enough short shots as it is. Complicating matters by trying to hit partial shots with more than one club is like throwing shots into the nearest water hazard. Work with one club—practice with it until you have confidence that you can hit any shot you need—and forget about all the others. Then and only then can you begin to integrate other clubs into your arsenal. You will find that knowing what club you are going to hit most of the time allows you to relax, clear your mind, and focus on the shot at hand.

EIGHT

○ ○ ○

"Don't You Wanna Play This Game No More"

This chapter title is from an Elton John song that my friend listens to on his iPod when he's practicing. It is also the perfect lead to a chapter dealing with moving off the driving range and venturing onto the golf course, where the game is actually played. One of the complaints I hear from players of all stripes is that they hit the ball great on the range—everything clicks and they feel great about their games—but the second they take the few short steps to the first tee, all the great swings flutter away in the breeze. These people call themselves "Roger Range Rats" or "Ranger Ricks," a moniker given to someone who looks ready for the Tour on the driving range but who can't play dead once he gets on the course.

Sadly, this malady is all too common. Players march from the driving range to the first tee thinking:

- If I can rotate my hands back behind me the way I was doing on the range, I won't slice my drives.

- And if I push off with my right big toe from the top of the backswing as I did with those wedges (okay, I only shanked three), I'll hit it close on number six.

- I drew that one 5-iron after hitting twenty cuts, so I ought to be able to turn it left into the pin on fourteen.

- What if I hit it this good on the golf course? Ohmygosh, I could have my best day ever!

- Of course, I've got to remember to put that little extra into my 3-wood the way I was doing toward the end of that practice session.

- And if I just pull my arms in close together right before I take the club back, I'll make a big full turn and hit it longer than I usually do—even though half those shots went forty yards right.

If you go to the tee with any of these swing thoughts, your round is done before you tee off. Besides, you go to the range to warm up before playing, not to work on your golf swing. Fortunately, this malady is curable, just not with your current practice habits.

Ben Hogan said that he never hit a shot on the course that he hadn't already hit a thousand times on the range, and he never hit a shot on the range that he would not need on the golf course. Likewise, Claude Harmon always told his kids that he "never hit a shot in practice that he wouldn't need on the back nine on Sunday." And Tiger Woods practiced hitting three-quarter knockdown 2-irons off tight lies for a year in preparation for the 2006 British Open (which he won hitting a lot of 2-irons). Jack Nicklaus used to hit thousands of high-drawing tee shots in practice (even though he normally played a fade), because he knew he would need to draw the ball on ten and seventeen at Augusta National the first week in April. Michael Jordan began practicing his unblockable turnaround fadeaway jumper well before he started using it on a regular basis, knowing he would need it later in his career as his overall athleticism declined.

Most amateurs hit balls for the sake of hitting balls, working on nothing specific in their swings, and never once thinking about what shots they might need during their next round. That sort of mindless ball-beating is not just a waste of time, it can actually be detrimental to your game. Or, if you happen to spend all your time during practice sessions thinking and working on your swing, you will do the same on the golf course. If you train your mind/body system to focus only on the mechanics of the golf swing while practicing, why wouldn't you integrate the same mind-set onto the course?

"UP, UP AND AWAY, IN MY BEAUTIFUL BALLOON"

The breezy lyrics of the Fifth Dimension classic are a perfect metaphor for what happens to most people at the driving range. You hit good shots in practice, all the while thinking that you're getting better. You're able to relax; you know you're not embarrassing yourself. Sure, not all the swings are perfect—you still top a few, and chunk a few, and hit a few low, screaming duds—but on the whole, you hit it okay. You might even whistle a tune while you work.

I hate to break the news to you, but if you're like many golfers, you are not practicing "golf" on the range, you are practicing "golf swing." Think about it: when was the last time you hit ten to twenty shots with the same club from a perfect lie on the golf course? Or what about having a bucket of balls full of "do-overs"? And then there's the wondrous 250-yard-wide fairway that is the driving range. What about the fact that when you play, you (not me, in a round of speed golf!) normally wait five to fifteen minutes between each shot, and that next one is played with a completely different club and from a completely different lie than the last one?

Then you get to the first tee, where you look at the hazard on your right, the out-of-bounds stakes on your left, the bunker looking like a sea of quicksand directly in your line of sight, and the small sliver of fairway that looks narrower than a bowling lane. Suddenly, the swing that felt so comfortable on the range vanishes like the girl in the magician's box. The quick, tense motion you have on the course sends the ball everywhere but the fairway, and you spend the day frustrated by how quickly you went from being a relatively decent ball striker to a complete hacker.

But how well were you hitting it on the range, really? Were you under any pressure? Of course not: you were trying to look pretty, making smooth swings, and occasionally succeeding. When you did fail and hit one sideways, there were no consequences. You simply raked over another ball. No big deal. You forgot about the last one and moved on.

Speed golf is the ultimate example of having mastered the necessary skills and then allowing things to happen, instinctively and intuitively, with no conscious thought when it's time to perform. In the words of former Masters and PGA Championship winner Jackie Burke Jr., "Your last thought before you take the club away isn't a thought at all but a feeling, a sensation, a generalized vision of the swing as a whole. If you interrupt that with a conscious thought, you're gone."

A lackadaisical approach to practice (which is all too common in golf) allows you to fool yourself into believing you're better than you are. It also lets you get away with what I call "balloon flaws" in your swing—flaws that inflate when you feel any pressure or get into a tight situation. On the range, you can get away with that loopy, quick-hands swing. Even if it looks like you're casting a fly-rod line into a trout stream, you still hit it okay on the range, because you are relaxed and your mind and body can compensate for your bad technique. Your overall level of caring is quite low. Once on the course, however, where you have to chase your own shots, and where one bad swing can lead to a double bogey, triple bogey, or worse, that swing flaw you were able to mask on the driving range grows like an inflating balloon.

The way to avoid those balloon flaws is to forge your swing under the same intense fire that you will experience on the golf course. You do that by changing the way you practice.

"UNTIL WE MAKE IT WORK, NOW LET'S MAKE IT HURT"

Busta Rhymes doesn't know Jackie Burke Jr., and vice versa. But the old Texas pro knows a thing or two about working till you make it hurt. Tour pro Billy Ray Brown once went to Houston for a putting lesson from Jackie. On the putting green, Billy Ray rolled a six-footer that missed the hole on the right side by a couple of inches. As he reached out to rake over another ball, Billy Ray glanced up just in time to see the palm of Jackie's hand heading toward his forehead. Jackie hit him between the eyes and almost knocked him down. Then he pointed a finger and yelled, "Billy Ray, I want it to *hurt* when you miss a putt."

I'm not advocating physical violence, but to improve the swing you carry to the golf course, you need to increase the intensity of your practice sessions.

This happens in other sports all the time. Two constants that came out of the Bear Bryant era at the University of Alabama were that Bear's teams were always national powerhouses, and the players always thought that the games were easy compared to the practices. Quarterback Kenny "The Snake" Stabler said, "We couldn't wait till Saturday. Compared to what we went through at practices all week the games were a piece of cake."

The same was true for most champions. Players on Bobby Knight's 1976 undefeated University of Indiana basketball team couldn't wait for the games, because the practices were so grueling. Rick Pitino's University of Kentucky basketball squads experienced much of the same pain in practices. The games were a relief. Jerome Bettis still says that the toughest workout he ever experienced was Lou Holtz's winter conditioning program during their championship run at Notre Dame. Emil Zátopek, the last man to win the 5K, 10K, and marathon in the same Olympics (Helsinki, 1952), used to train with army boots on his feet and his wife on his shoulders! How do you think he felt when he put on a pair of running shoes and shorts?

Bryant also told his players that they could improve 5 percent a day if they only worked at it. According to Ozzie Newsome, "He said the same thing was true for anybody, like a doctor or a lawyer; and that was his way to make sure a player didn't become complacent and rest on his laurels. I took that to heart. I don't think there's any doubt learning that from him at Alabama made me a better pro with the Cleveland Browns."

It will make you a better golfer if you take it to heart as well.

"BLAME IT ON THE RAIN"

I use a Milli Vanilli reference because I want you to work on golf's equivalent of lip-synching. Some of the best and most effective practice time you can have will be making swings in slow motion without a golf ball. It is also the one task I recommend that earns the most groans. "It's boring," most people say, or, "I know I can swing the club without the ball; it's hitting the ball that's the problem." All these complaints are true, and all are irrelevant.

Mastering the skills is the first step; otherwise swing thoughts and conscious how-to thoughts are inevitable. There are many important aspects to building the necessary skills, but arguably the single most important factor in learning to control a golf ball is time. It also happens to be the one element people don't seem to have enough of in today's world. The human body and psyche are not pieces of modern technology and do not increasingly do things faster.

Neurologists and repetitive-motion specialists have proven that the best learning occurs when results are removed (e.g., the screen and the keys are covered when you're learning to type) and when the motion is repeated numerous times in extra-slow motion.

Time is truly of the essence in mastering the art and science of hitting a golf ball, as well as learning to play the game of golf. The two, in fact, are not one and the same. Although striking a golf ball is part of playing golf, it is but a piece of the puzzle of overall performance. Far too much instruction and practice today focus solely on building a better (or, heaven forbid, perfect) full swing. This idea ignores all the other crucial elements of shooting lower scores.

Time on task builds what I call "The Big E," Experience. A master of anything is first a master of learning. And experience comes solely from having done something optimally, many, many times.

According to K. Anders Ericsson, a professor of psychology at Florida State University, talent is the result of a single process— deliberate practice, which he defines as "individuals engaging in a practice activity (typically designed by coaches) with full concentration on improving some aspect of their performance." Ericsson has devoted much of his life to studying talented performers and has come up with a formula known as the Power Law of Learning: $T = aP - b$. In a layperson's terms, it can be translated as "practice means working on technique (specific and functional to the individual), seeking constant and critical feedback and focusing ruthlessly on improving weaknesses."

This sounds strikingly similar to the Laws of Learning that John Wooden, arguably the greatest coach of all time, stressed in building skills in his players and winning NCAA championships. According to the Wizard of Westwood, those laws are as follows:

- Explanation

- Demonstration

- Imitation

- Correction (when necessary—and it usually is)

- Repetition

Wooden was adamant about the quality of the time spent learning: "Activity—to produce real results—must be organized and executed meticulously." When I'm preparing for a speed-golf event, I practice the specific shots with the specific clubs I expect to use on the golf course. This is particularly important when only carrying a few clubs. I may have to hit a 120-yard 8-iron that spins slightly from left to right, or a 5-iron that flies low for 160 yards with a little draw spin on it. This is a precise, detailed, and focused manner of practicing.

What John Wooden is to college basketball, Larisa Preobrazhenskaya is to professional women's tennis in its present-day hotbed, the Spartak Tennis Club outside of Moscow. By the beginning of 2007, Russian women accounted for fully half of the top ten female players in the world and twelve of the top fifty. Something is going on there, just as it is in South Korea with women golfers, the Dominican Republic and Venezuela when it comes to major-league baseball players, and many of us when we first play a round of speed golf. Something is working.

Preobrazhenskaya and Wooden share some interesting commonalities in their coaching and learning processes. I've found much the same success with many of my students when it comes to building a new motion, a process that takes patience, fundamentals, and discipline. Preobrazhenskaya's youngsters play many games without tennis balls, sometimes in slow motion, imitating the correct motions, even down to the footwork. When necessary, Preobrazhenskaya steps in and corrects, placing the body or racket in the desired position. All this is done with one goal in mind: learn to hit the tennis ball clean and hard—good impact. The tennis ball is much like the golf ball in this way; it only knows physics. It doesn't care who you are, how much money you make, or what kind of car you drive. The ball only knows how the tool (racket or clubface/clubhead) is being applied to the backside of it.

Wooden applied similar tactics at UCLA when he made his teams practice and play basketball without the ball. Without the basketball, there are no baskets or rebounds. Without those distractions, Wooden's players were better able to devote their full attention to the other fundamentals. "For a player, the basketball is like catnip to a cat—irresistible," Wooden said. "So I occasionally started practice without a basketball on the court. Players ran patterns and executed moves without having to worry about the ball. Forcing them to make imaginary passes helped to instill good habits and improve timing, footwork, elbow and hand position, and balance."

Your golf ball creates as many distractions as the basketball did for Wooden's championship UCLA teams. The impulse to hit or lift the ball is a detriment to learning to swing in a different— and in most cases, more efficient—way. In learning to master your new optimal swing, I want you to slow down, as mentioned previously, and focus all your attention on your fundamental, ideal motion. The body doesn't know whether there is a ball there or not, so from a physiological point of view the correct repetition work is being done.

"Yeah, yeah, yeah, but how do I take that solid shot I was hitting on the range with me to the first tee? And how do I do it right now?"

Since this is the bubble-bursting section of the book, let me dispel a cruel myth. Progress in golf is often marketed and sold as something you can have in a day, a week, or six months. Unfortunately, that is snake oil. As with any skill, the time you spend on task is the only thing that will make you a better player.

If you decide one day that you want to learn to play the piano, competent teachers will give you this scenario, which is considered quite normal for learning to play the piano or other musical instrument: one lesson a week for five years, with at least one hour of practice every day in between the lessons. If you cannot commit to this, they will not accept you as a student. Most will also give you a cloth keyboard to practice your fingering techniques: one that gives off no sound at all. If practicing on a silent keyboard makes you a better pianist, and practicing basketball without a ball makes you one of the greatest dynasties of all time, why wouldn't practicing golf without a golf ball help you build a better swing?

The personal swing you are building will not be completed in a day, a week, or a month. When, with Butch Harmon's help, Tiger Woods changed his swing the first time (after the 1997 Masters), Tiger didn't get completely comfortable with the changes until mid-1999, close to two years after the decision to change was made. And Tiger was hitting upward of five hundred practice balls a day. Perhaps more important, the balls he was hitting were with the new motion, as opposed to banging balls and continuing to ingrain the old, undesirable one, which is what happens with most amateurs.

Of course, we know how Tiger's changes worked out. But how many of you would have the patience to work on something every day for two and a half years before you saw positive results? My guess is, not many.

If standing in front of a mirror practicing different swing positions in super slow motion doesn't sound like much fun—too bad. Students who do this sort of practice make far bigger changes and improvements in their golf swing than those who hit a lot of balls. In front of your mirror you can monitor your motion step by step (due to the slowness) and ensure that you are building and repeating the correct motion. When you hit golf balls, particularly with a full swing at full speed, even though you may be trying to make a new and improved motion, you normally continue to make the old swing, the one that doesn't travel well from the driving range to the first tee.

You think doing slow swings without a ball is torturous? Preobrazhenskaya's students are not permitted to play a tournament for the first three years of study. She believes wholly in developing the proper fundamentals without distractions. There's no doubt that Preobrazhenskaya is familiar with an old Russian proverb: "Repetition is the mother of learning."

Coach Wooden also stressed that "a good demonstration is better than a great explanation." Although an explanation provides information and knowledge, visual images are what the brain actually sees. Everything in our world that is now "real" was first an image; let us not forget that there was a time when no words existed.

Professor Ericsson also discusses the Ten Year Rule, an intriguing finding dating to 1899, which shows that even the most talented individual requires a decade of committed practice before reaching world-class level. Chess prodigy Bobby Fischer put in nine hard years before achieving his grand-master status at age sixteen; it is speculated that by the time Mozart was six, he had studied some thirty-five hundred hours of music with his father; and ball handler supreme Pistol Pete Maravich had a basketball at his side—all the time, practically everywhere—for well more than a decade before he arrived at LSU and bedazzled fans with his skills.

"But, Christopher," you say, "what about the true geniuses, the savants?" Although they excel within narrow domains that feature clear, logical rules, their true expertise, research suggests, is in their ability to practice obsessively, even when it doesn't look as if they're practicing. As Ericsson puts it, "There's no cell type that geniuses have that the rest of us don't." Mozart practiced so often that his fingers were crooked at a young age; Eric Clapton practiced until his fingers bled on a daily basis; and Wynton Marsalis practices five to eight hours every single day. So, what came first, genius or a devoted and focused work ethic?

Coach Wooden, Larisa Preobrazhenskaya, Bear Bryant, and other great coaches obviously knew what they were doing, whether or not they understood the science behind their success. From a neuroscience standpoint, these coaches were building something called *myelin* in their players. Myelin is a layer of fat wrapped around nerve fibers like rubber insulation on a wire. This myelin keeps the nerve signals strong by preventing electrical impulses from leaking out.

Myelin gets thicker as the nerve is stimulated, and practicing a repetitive motion, whether it's a ground stroke in tennis, a pick-and-roll in basketball, a cross block in football, or your golf swing in front of a mirror, allows the nerve signals to travel faster and more accurately, which leads to better timing. Through repetition, the myelin sheath is thickened and the circuitry between your muscles and brain is strengthened. This is crucial to learning, because your brain alone won't get the job done. As mentioned earlier, scientists have determined that our five senses are taking in more than eleven million pieces of information every second. The eyes alone receive and send over ten million signals to the brain. The most liberal estimates of how many signals can be processed in the conscious mind is forty bits of information per second. Think about it: we take in eleven million pieces of information, but can only process forty of them consciously. The other 10,999,960 are stored in the subconscious, to be used when called upon, as when you turn off your brain before swinging the golf club. Optimum performance is allowed to happen, not caused. In addition, let us not forget that the conscious mind has no experience—it's never "done" anything—leaving the subconscious mind, with all its past experience, to take the lead.

If we think now of the best in the business, Tiger Woods, we may begin to see part of his genius. Tiger started swinging a club at age two (his very first swings were, interestingly enough, left-handed) under the competent supervision of his father. So he has been myelinating his golf-swing circuitry for nearly thirty years. And in those thirty years, he has spent immeasurable quality hours building, through correct repetition and expert coaching and instruction, the motions and positions he desires in his swing (Tiger, by the way, does a lot of practice in slow motion and without a ball). Is it Tiger's protoplasm that allows him to swing the way he does? Partially, but then again, his parents always told him, "You'll get out of it whatever you put into it."

You can improve your golf swing without going to a practice facility or golf course and without hitting a ball. Think about the money you'll save on range balls! And the time and fuel you'll conserve in not having to drive somewhere to practice your golf swing. If you're truly interested in building a better swinging motion, get rid of the ball, slow down, have competent (a mirror or credible coach) feedback, and begin to myelinate the nerve fibers devoted to your golf swing.

Why don't more golfers move off the range and into their bedrooms where the full-length mirror resides? My take is that most people lack the discipline to take the ball away, and even more believe (wrongly) that they understand intellectually and conceptually what they are attempting to do, so they can avoid all this mind-body-neuron nonsense. I'm sure that's what most of Coach Wooden's players thought when they showed up at UCLA and had their basketballs taken away, but

Christopher checking his setup and preparing to make a full swing in slow motion in front of a mirror.

his teams won ten championships in twelve years.

Robert Lansdorp, a tennis coach in Los Angeles, echoes those thoughts. Lansdorp has coached former number-one-ranked players Pete Sampras, Tracy Austin, and Lindsay Davenport, all three of whom grew up playing at the same run-of-the-mill tennis clubs near Los Angeles.

"You need fundamentals and discipline—not a fancy academy—and in this country nobody gives a damn about fundamentals and discipline," Lansdorp says.

The same is true in golf. Building the swing is the easy part (really); playing the game of golf is the true test. I believe it has become increasingly challenging due to today's practice habits. In fact, many players spend most or all of their precious time on building their golf swing but neglect training "in context," or specific to what a round of golf requires.

For me to replicate a round of speed golf, there is only one way to do so: go play a round of speed golf. Yes, I can practice quickly selecting a club on the range and firing a shot at a target while my heart rate is elevated, but it's not quite the same as when it's happening on the course. And in my run training for speed golf, I can certainly do intervals, which I perform on a regular basis, to simulate the stopping and starting involved in a round of speed golf.

What I've described above is sports-specific training for my chosen form of golf. What I see most players practicing has nothing to do with what is transpiring on a golf course. In fact, if you have ever spent a period of time when you've practiced more and have not seen your score go down, you too may have been a victim of ineffective or poor practice.

"GAMES PEOPLE PLAY"

Ever wonder why all those teaching aids never seem to work? In theory, they all should train your body to do specific things. Those connection vests should train you to keep your upper arms against your body; the hinged clubs should get you swinging on the correct plane; the wooden tracks along the ground should keep you moving the putter down the target line through impact; and those nifty fans on the end of the shafts should help you feel a proper release. So why don't they? Why don't people who work with all those gizmos improve faster than those who don't?

Although many teaching aids allow you to capture a certain picture or feeling, either visually or kinesthetically, the swings you make with them do not fire the nerves in the same patterns as when they are not present. Even hitting a ball off an uneven lie forces the nerves and muscles to react very differently from that perfectly flat one you find on the driving range mat. Training aids are like crutches, which will make you mobile but won't teach you how to run again. The more you rely on the teaching aids, the more dependent you become on the crutch. Each and every golf swing is unique in a multitude of aspects—club, distance to be covered, slope, and lie of ball, to mention a few—and thus must be practiced and learned accordingly. And no matter how long and hard you work with them, the minute you put the aid down and head to the course, you will more often than not revert back to your old golf swing. Use training aids briefly and sparingly— then discard and replicate the conditions of on-course play.

A fun photo of Christopher using a multitude of teaching gizmos, like something out of *Tin Cup*.

Playing golf requires problem solving and decision making in reaction to ever-changing conditions. Most training aids are aimed at fixing and are not geared toward proactive learning. Plus, last I checked, training aids were not allowed on the golf course. Additionally, proponents of discovery learning contend that you acquire and retain skills best when your mind plays an active role in figuring out how to perform them. When using a training aid, the mind is not engaged: you might be thinking about what you are going to have for lunch, since a training aid is doing all the work.

"You should be suspicious of training aids that promise muscle memory, because the term itself is a misnomer," says Mark Guadagnoli, professor of kinesiology at the University of Nevada–Las Vegas. "Muscles can't be trained through repetitive motion, as marketers of some products suggest. The neurons in the brain tell the muscles what to do. When we practice, certain neurons get used to working together; but unless the golfer is cognitively engaged, no real learning can occur."

The human memory system is designed to flush things. When you say a phone number over and over, and then dial it, you probably forget it almost immediately. When you cram for a test, you remember the info just long enough to get through the class. A year later, you couldn't pass that test on a bet. The same thing happens when you strap on a training aid and plow through a bucket of balls. Creating a great golf swing is like finding a needle in a field of haystacks. A training aid might point you to the right haystack, but it cannot find the needle for you. Aids will give you the feel for what you're trying to do, but the shots you hit with them are not authentic golf swings. Keep that in mind, and use these aids sparingly if at all.

Who better to consider when it comes to the value of training aids than the baron of practice himself—Ben Hogan. Did the man who claimed that the "secret" was "in the dirt" ever use training aids? According to his former caddie, Jody Vasquez, Hogan never used any sort of teaching/training aid. "I offered him a putting device once," Vasquez said. "He tried it a few times and quickly discarded it. Mr. Hogan's philosophy was to go out and hit 10,000 balls. If after 10,000 balls you hadn't figured it out, you probably needed to take up tennis."

Doc Farnsworth echoes many of the same sentiments: "Training aids are overutilized, and when they are used, they are often misused. You have to be engaged and looking for feedback when using a training aid, and there must be a certain amount of discipline in its use." The consensus, then, is that training aids must be used carefully, sparingly, and periodically; otherwise, they may be detrimental and a waste of your precious time.

Here is a practice game that will intensify your workout and simulate the pressure you will feel on the golf course. First pick a target and the type of shot you want to hit. If it's a soft-cut 7-iron, be very specific about where you want the ball to land and where you want it to end up. Then draw a twenty-foot circle around that spot. If you are at a modern practice facility, that circle could be drawn for you in the form of a target green. If not, you will have to be creative in drawing an imaginary circle around where you want the ball to end up.

Then pull out five practice balls and hit the shot you have

chosen five times. But if you miss your target circle with one shot, you have to add two balls to your pile. Thus if you miss the twenty-foot circle with your first ball, you add two, leaving you with six balls in your pile. Miss the next one, and you have seven balls in your pile. If you hit four good ones in a row, but miss on the fifth, you have to add two more balls. You can spend hours on this game before you finally run out of balls. And there is no greater pressure than getting down to that last ball and having to make one more good swing to eliminate the pile.

If you just want to score better on the course you play regularly, play the five-ball game with the clubs and shots that you have to hit on the par threes at your course. The shot you choose might depend slightly on course conditions and where the tee markers and hole placements are on a particular day, but you should have a pretty good idea of what club you will be swinging and what kind of shot you need to hit. Rehearsing those shots will make them seem easier once you are faced with the real thing on the course. And once you are comfortable hitting all the par threes, you will see your scores tumble.

When you're confident that you can hit the par threes with some regularity, you should play the five-ball game with the tee shots you will need for the par fours and fives. If it's necessary to hit a driver on all the fours and fives, pick a ball flight that you can reproduce consistently and build an imaginary fairway on the driving range between flags or markers. If you don't need a driver, practice with a 3-wood, hybrid, or long iron, so you'll be ready when it's time to hit the shot.

Improving off the tee and on par threes will have drastic results on your score. Playing the five-ball game will put a lot of pressure on your swing, exactly the kind of thing you will feel when you migrate from the range to the golf course.

So many different conditions present themselves in a round of golf, yet most players spend vast amounts of time hitting full

7-irons off a flat, artificial surface. Then they wonder why, when they have a three-quarter 7-iron shot off a slight sidehill lie and the ball is sitting down in the grass, they can't pull the shot off. Well, it's simple: if you haven't practiced a specific shot, your mind and body will not be able to execute it. A round of golf is not like shooting a free throw or throwing a dart, motions that are more or less the same every time. So why do we practice them as such?

Major champions don't. In 1993, when Greg Norman showed up at Royal St. George's, he was hitting balls on the range when he realized that there was not a single shot on the golf course that resembled the smooth, flat surface of the range. So he moved off to the right—well right—of the equipment trailers that lined the boundaries of the range, and hit towering 5-irons off all kinds of sidehill, downhill, and uphill lies. This caused a mild crisis when one of the tournament officials from the R&A (the rules body and organizer of the tournament) told Greg that he needed to move back to the range. Greg said no and told the official that if the R&A wanted to rescind his invitation, fine, but the side of the range was the only place where he could get his work done.

The R&A let Greg play, and he shot 64 on Sunday in a thirty-knot wind to win his second British Open Championship. Butch Harmon still calls it the best major championship round he has ever seen (and Butch has seen a lot of good ones). And it all started with Greg being the only player in the field with the fore-sight to find a practice spot that simulated the lies he would find on the golf course.

"SO IF YOU WANNA PLAY, THEN LET'S PLAY"

Obviously, the best place to practice golf is on the golf course. Go to the United Kingdom and ask for a bag of balls and directions to the driving range, and the folks behind the counter will look at you as though you're French. There is no driving range. So if a golfer wants to "practice," there is only one place to do it: the golf course. Not so long ago, all golf lessons were given on the course, for there was no alternative. And although there may have been discussion of the golf swing, the lesson automatically stressed the playing of the game. When someone comes to me seeking assistance, I always ask if he or she wants a "golf-swing lesson" or a "golf lesson." If you want a golf lesson, there's only one place to take it—on the golf course.

Only on the course can you truly encounter the myriad different situations and conditions that arise in a round, plus all the other components of playing good golf, which include the mental situations and course-management sides of the game. There are plenty of games you can play with yourself on the course that will help you improve when the time comes for you to be under the gun.

Other than running between shots, what are some ways that you can make your training and practice regimes harder, so the game might seem easier?

"OLD SCHOOL"

- Today's club technology feels like cheating. Forgiveness and ease is what we all want when it's time to perform, but in training, why not make it harder? Put an old, small-headed persimmon driver in your bag, or even a small-headed fairway wood, and find a set of forged blades (yeah, the ones that look like butter knives) along with a straight-edged "bull's-eye" putter. Set the lies and lofts of your irons to the same specs as your "gamers" and get ready for some serious feedback on your mis-hits. Then dig up some beat-up golf balls, and go practice and play. Your modern, high-tech equipment will look and feel pretty sweet when you go back to it.

"GONNA BE BAD FOR GOOD"

- On the putting green, stop hitting three balls to the same hole from the same distance. When was the last time you got three chances at the same putt on the golf course? If you are warming up, fine, but when you're practicing, take one ball and simulate some of the putts you will likely have on the golf course.

  Then play eighteen holes on the practice putting green. Keep score with all the holes being par twos. Find some other people practicing their putting and challenge them to a little match. These are simple ways to make you feel the way you do on the golf course. And if you want to re-create that nervous feeling you get over a short putt, try running fifty yards out and back, and then hit a putt. Or drop on the ground and do ten or twenty slow push-ups prior to hitting that nasty four-footer (or use the push-ups as a "pain penalty" if you miss the four-footer). If you really need to work on your putting stroke, head back to your favorite padded cell with the specific purpose in mind, and work until you get the form right.

- Play a round of golf at the driving range. Imagine every hole and what club/shot would be required. Go through your preshot routine and "play" the result. If possible, change the lie of the ball to simulate different fairway conditions. Hit short shots if you believe you may have missed the green with your approach, and putt out (normally there is a practice green in the vicinity). Also, try taking a few minutes (more time!) between each shot—that's what happens on the course; you're not hitting one shot immediately after the other. Standing there hitting twenty consecutive drivers, pitches, or 5-irons off a perfectly flat surface might build confidence, but it is not practicing golf.

From time to time, take a seat, close your eyes, and visualize or picture your desired golf swing, shot result, or even how you want to play a particular hole or course. The nonconscious doesn't know the difference between real and imagined, hence the power of visualization. Building healthy and positive unconscious patterns—since our lives are basically run by our unconscious—is as important as building a good golf swing.

- If you are stuck hitting balls off a flat, artificial surface, practice hitting different golf shots: draws, fades, low, and high. Learn to make one club go different distances. Hit your 7-iron 150 yards at varied trajectories, curve it from right to left, then from left to right. Then do the same thing at 125 yards, 100 yards, 75 yards, and 50 yards. This will enhance your creativity and imagination and provide feedback that is critical for learning that lasts. I see kids do this quite frequently—without being asked. They find it fun and challenging, much more entertaining than trying to hit twenty-five consecutive "perfect" 5-irons.

- When practicing around the green, throw balls all over the place, on different slopes and on varied lies. That's what's going to happen on the golf course, so if you haven't specifically practiced the situation, don't expect to succeed when faced with it under the gun of actual play. Failure to prepare is preparing to fail.

- Best-ball formats make the game easier, because you have a partner who can bail you out when you hit it in the trees or when you can't get out of that pesky bunker. But best balls do nothing to improve your game. So instead play eighteen holes of "worst ball." Hit two balls for each shot, always selecting the worse one. If you bomb your first drive down the middle of the fairway, tee up another and take the worse. If you make a thirty-footer on your first attempt, put down another ball and try it again, playing the ball that ends up farther from the hole. Playing with one ball will seem like a relief after experiencing a few of the horrors of worst ball.

"YOU'RE THE ONLY ONE FOR ME"

One of my favorite and mandatory practice games for those big hitters who tend to accrue masses of penalty strokes due to lost balls is to have those folks tee off with only one ball in their bags. That's right, one. When you lose it, you walk in: no excuses. This is the ultimate test in controlling your golf ball and managing the golf course. Knowing you have a couple of spare sleeves in your bag will ease your mind after a few rounds of playing with just one.

"RAIN COME DOWN"

Go play in the ugliest, cruelest, coldest, hottest, rainiest, and windiest conditions you can find. Fair-weather golfers avoid such situations at all costs. If you're looking to improve your golf game, go seek them out.

The best in the world do. When Annika Sörenstam was growing up in Sweden, she was at her course one day when it started to rain. As always, she called her father to come pick her up. But as they were driving away, both glanced out the car window and saw several girls hitting balls in a downpour. That is when Annika's father said, "You know, Annika, there are no shortcuts."

She still gets tears in her eyes as she tells that story. And she still hits balls in the nastiest weather conditions she can find.

If you do the same, you might feel like you're playing from the up tees next time a warm, calm, seventy-five-degree day rolls around.

"SEND IN THE CLOWNS"

Try playing a few holes on just one leg or with only one hand on the club. Leo Diegel, who won back-to-back PGA Championships in 1928 and 1929, could shoot around par on one leg. Although the nerves and muscles that are firing will be different from those used during your traditional swing, you will be very appreciative next time you have both hands on the club and both feet on the ground.

"LESS IS MORE"

Try playing with half a tool set, or take out all the even- or all the odd-numbered clubs. Or take out all but one of your wedges. Take the driver out of the bag for a round or two, and see what you shoot. Would you really make a lot of big numbers if your ball was in the fairway 200 yards out every time? Remove your putter and roll the ball with something else, like a fairway metal, hybrid, or that lonely wedge. If you find that tough, good, because your full set will look beautiful when you put all your clubs back in the bag.

Out of boredom—or perhaps sheer madness—I occasionally play nine holes with just a 5-iron, running between shots (I once shot one over par on the back nine at the Ghost Creek course at Pumpkin Ridge in a little over eighteen minutes). That sort of round makes your five-hour round with all those clubs seem like a different sport.

I once shot 73 at the Eastmoreland Golf Club, here in the Portland area, site of the 1990 U.S. Public Links Championship—with just a 5-iron. Thad Taber, the only six-time World One-Club Champion, shot 69 in competition with only a 6-iron. Give it a try sometime. After you do, having fourteen clubs in the bag will make the game seem awfully easy the next time you play.

All these forms of training stretch you beyond your comfort zone. To grow, learn, and progress, in whatever endeavor, you have to escape your cozy element and challenge your mind and body to reach their full potential.

WHAT YOU CAN LEARN FROM SPEED GOLF

Since I started playing speed golf, "normal" golf now seems too easy to me—like cheating. My heart rate is not elevated, and I've got all the time in the world to calculate my exact yardage and take a little longer look at my putting line. Playing with fourteen clubs seems downright unfair after having played with only six. I might even do a little rehearsal swing or two from around the green to get a feel for what sort of swing I want to take, or take an extra moment to read the green. Speed golf has made traditional golf seem, to borrow a phrase from *Caddyshack*'s Carl Spackler after he wielded high-powered artillery in his plight against Bushwood's troublesome gophers, "like gravy."

NINE

O O O

"Give Me the Strength, So I Can Help You"

Phil Collins, whose lyrics I lifted for the title of this chapter, has been known to hit a golf ball pretty well, but he is not what you would call a "strong" player. In that regard, he's not alone. Few of the amateurs I see would be characterized as strong or athletic. Some were decent athletes in their teenage years, but that was thirty pounds and two surgeries ago, or something to that effect. Today most of the people I teach subscribe to the John Daly approach: if you can smoke and drink while you play, it can't be much of an athletic endeavor.

I disagree with that and have a lot of empirical evidence to back up my side of the argument. And besides, when it comes to the specific types of athletic traits necessary to play good golf, Daly has no shortage, nor do Craig Stadler and Tim Herron. Golf is indeed an athletic sport; it may not be as athletically demanding as an Iron Man triathlon or a lacrosse doubleheader, but it is more physically challenging than darts or billiards. And even though you can, indeed, have a cigar and a beer during your round, you will shoot lower scores and enjoy the game a lot more if you treat golf as a sport that you condition and train your body to play.

By "conditioning" I mean getting stronger, more flexible, and in better shape—strength training, cardiovascular workouts, and getting down on the floor and stretching muscles you never knew you had. If you do this, you will hit the golf ball farther, straighter, and more consistently; your overall short game and putting will be better; and you will have more energy and focus in the late stages of your rounds.

The physical demands speed golf puts on me are apparent; being able to control a golf ball while combating fatigue and an elevated heart rate, with only a handful of clubs, requires superior mental and physical conditioning. The better my physical conditioning, the less recovery time I need, and the faster I can run while still hitting quality golf shots. Being fit is paramount for speed golfers, and it has become much the same for the best players in the world. If you are truly interested in shooting lower scores and improving overall golf performance, you need to follow suit, regardless of your present level of play.

Tour players know the importance of conditioning; other than the practice tee, the busiest place on tour in the late afternoons is the fitness trailer. Personal trainers are as prevalent as swing coaches, and all players stick to their individual exercise regimens as closely as they stick to their tee times. This is a relatively new phenomenon on tour. Johnny Revolta, winner of the 1935 PGA Championship, once lit up a Lucky Strike during a round and overheard a man in the gallery say, "I've never seen an athlete smoke during a game before." Revolta turned to the guy and snapped, "You still haven't. I'm not an athlete; I'm a golfer."

The best players in the world, including Jack Nicklaus and Arnold Palmer, used to scoff at Gary Player when he traveled with dumbbells in his luggage. Player, the godfather of the modern golf fitness movement, would always find the local gym in whatever town he was visiting, and, despite snickers from his fellow players, he never missed a chance to preach the benefits of being in great shape. Some players were downright hostile to Gary's thinking. When he was in his prime, Johnny Miller scoffed at lifting weights, saying that doing so built too much bulk and would hurt the golf swing.

Turns out Gary Player was right all along. And even though most players of the past were more likely to lift a highball glass than a dumbbell, the truly great ones possessed strength, flexibility, and muscular control and coordination specific and beneficial to golf. Sam Snead was a physical freak with the strength and flexibility of a Cirque de Soleil performer—he could keep one foot flat on the floor and kick the top of a door frame, a parlor trick he displayed well into his sixties. The Slammer could also pluck a ball out of the hole without bending his knees; Ben Hogan was incredibly flexible and had phenomenal reflexes, which saved his life in 1950 when he was almost killed in a car crash; Palmer and Nicklaus were both physically strong; Mickey Wright, whose golf swing Hogan declared was "the best I've ever seen," was an imposing physical presence and a powerful ball striker; and Babe Zaharias, the founder of the LPGA, was an Olympic track and field medalist. Although players of yesteryear may have built their physical prowess through more "natural" means (and of course some level of athleticism can always be attributed to genes), they were strong, flexible, powerful, quick, and in better condition than the average citizen of their day.

Today's top players are world-class athletes. If you ever saw Tiger Woods working out and didn't know who he was, you wouldn't be able to tell if he was a golfer, an NFL defensive back, a World Cup skier, or maybe some guy who wanted to look good for the ladies. His body type definitely does not scream "golfer." Annika Sörenstam totally transformed her body before becoming one of the greatest players in the history of women's golf. Her workout includes a thousand crunches a day, weight training, and hours on an elliptical trainer and exercise bike. Larry Nelson spent a year and a half working on his physical conditioning before heading to the Champions Tour. When he got there, he said that at age fifty he was in the best shape of his life, including the time he'd spent as an army sergeant.

Those players did pretty well when they improved their conditioning. While you may not reach their level, you will lower your scores if you get in better shape.

"WHY I WORK SO HARD FOR YOU"

Just when you think it can't get worse, I dig out the Wham! lyrics.

But I know what you're thinking: "Oh, no, not another 'hit the gym and get abs of steel to hit it farther' spiel. Why can't I sit here and eat Cheetos and learn how to play?" Well, for starters, every muscle in your body contracts during a golf swing. Some contract more than others, but you use every muscle in your body to hit a golf ball. If some of those muscles aren't up to the task, you won't hit it well. Jack Nicklaus used to lament about this problem all the time. "Why would I tell someone 'you need to add more leg drive to your swing' when the poor guy sits behind a desk all week and doesn't have any leg drive to give?" Jack asked. "It's a shame, but a lot of people just don't have the physical assets needed to make good golf swings."

Jack was right. While you don't have to be a bodybuilder to swing a golf club, a stronger, fitter person is going to generate more clubhead speed and adapt his or her swing faster than the person who has never lifted a weight and considers the exercise bike a great place to pile the laundry. There is no doubt that (whether chemically generated or not) Barry Bonds generated more bat speed and efficiency after gaining thirty pounds of muscle, LeBron James improved his outside shot after he hit the weight room, and Vijay Singh became the number-one golfer in the world after building a 4,000-square-foot gym next to his house and working out with a trainer six days a week.

Strength is not the only thing that improves with conditioning. Being in better shape improves your ability to repeat complex neuromuscular movements like the golf swing. So not only will you hit farther if you get stronger and fitter, you will gain more consistency in your swing. You will also chip and putt better. Ever wonder why women, in general, don't pitch, chip, and putt better than men? Pitches, chips, and putts are small motions that don't seem to require a great deal of speed or brute strength. Given the work ethic of professionals on both the men's and women's Tours, it would seem logical that LPGA pros would have short-game statistics similar to their counterparts on the PGA Tour. But it's not even close. PGA Tour pros' up-and-down percentage is a lot better than that of the best women players in the world, just as the best male players at your club probably chip, pitch, and putt better than the women's club champion. This is not a slap at the work ethic or practice habits of women: it is a biological fact of life. Men are, on average, 30 to 40 percent stronger than women. That added strength, particularly in the hands and forearms, gives men a natural advantage, even in the areas where strength doesn't appear to be a factor. Being stronger improves your tweezer dexterity, your quickness (even on short strokes like pitches and bunker shots), and your overall control of the clubhead and allows you to make swings with less effort and fatigue, all of which translate to a better short game.

"WHAT DO I HAVE TO DO?"

So what golf-specific exercises do you need to improve your game? Well, the first thing you need to do is forget that you ever put the words *golf* and *specific* together in the same sentence. I think "golf-specific" is a term that has been used and misused a lot in recent years. I hate to burst everyone's golf-fitness bubble, but the only motion and exercise that is truly golf-specific is hitting a golf ball. All that other golf-specific stuff is just so much hooey. Yes, you may strengthen and stretch muscles and parts of your body that are more active in a golf swing than they are when you're sitting and drinking a cup of coffee in the morning, but does that make those actions golf-specific?

According to physiotherapist Donn Dimond, "Golf fitness is any type of physical activity that will increase your ability to play golf. Based on this definition, there are many things that could be considered golf fitness. For one person this may mean just walking around the block a couple of times to increase his endurance if this person leads a sedentary life. For another person it may mean a very specific training program that incorporates strength and mobility. Golf fitness essentially comes down to what part of the body system you need to train to help your game; this system will vary among people."

That sounds a lot like what I've been preaching throughout these pages. Just reread what I've said about the grip, the setup, your backswing, impact, putting, balance, partial shots, and playing the game. There is no one way to do anything in golf, including exercising. I could tell you to do crunches six days a week, run a mile a day with interval sprints, lift weights for half an hour a day three days a week, do yoga, jump rope, work on your core muscles, do back exercises on a physioball, and use elastic bands to add resistance as you simulate your golf swing. But there is no need for me to go through all those exercises—there are entire books devoted to getting yourself in shape to play better golf—and if you did half of what I just listed, you would probably be bedridden for a month.

That is why I won't recommend any specific workout programs. For some of you, a brisk walk around the block will be an improvement over your current exercise regimen; others might need to mix up cardio and strength training; for still others, adding a stretching routine into a current workout mix will do the trick. What I can tell you is that, just as none of you swing the club the same as everyone else, the physical conditioning program you choose will be different from everyone else's.

So how does one build up effective and efficient golf-specific neuromuscular patterns? The answer is simple: hit more golf balls. But to be physically able to hit large numbers of golf balls, or just make many golf swings, you must be reasonably fit. Hence, one of the foremost goals of fitness for golf must be to prevent injury.

"The reason most people want to perform a golf fitness program is to primarily increase their ability to perform on the golf course and secondarily to increase their overall health," Dimond adds. "By making small increases in the amount of physical stress that your body can handle through training, you will increase your performance on the golf course."

Physical therapist Randy Ziobro, who received specialized training in strength and conditioning through the MedX company, which was founded by Arthur Jones, the creator of Nautilus, advises you to ask yourself a few questions before embarking on a physical fitness program. Those include:

- Do injuries limit your ability to play golf?

- For someone your age, do you consider yourself to be strong? Would others agree with that assessment?

- Are you weak?

- Are you flexible?

- Do you feel tight before, during, or after you play?

- Do you get fatigued from minimal amounts of exercise?

- Do you warm up before you play golf?

- Do you work out at the gym? At home? At all?

- Is fitness important to you or only important for improving your golf game?

- Will you exercise on your own?

"YOU DON'T CARE THAT YOU HURT ME"

I don't mind using Justin Timberlake lyrics at all. Not only is Justin a cool guy, he loves his golf and is in phenomenal shape. But while he didn't mean for his words to be used for this purpose, "You don't care that you hurt me" would be the perfect thing to say to the game. Golf doesn't give two whits about whether you injure yourself hitting balls. And it is very easy to do. Lower-back, wrist, elbow, neck, shoulder, and knee injuries are common among golfers, even more so among those who are carrying a few extra pounds and who haven't worked out in years.

While nothing will completely eliminate the possibility of injury, warming up—and I mean good, long warm-ups before hitting your first shot—will diminish your chances of hobbling off the course and spending the weekend flat on your back. All top-level athletes warm up, yet golfers often jump out of their cars, after having been sedentary at their desks in front of their computers for hours, make a few practice swings, and head to the first tee. You might as well tell the game, "Hurt me now, and, oh by the way, ruin my score while you're at it."

"Although there is strong evidence to support warming up, the majority of golfers do not do it," Dimond claims. "In one research study, over one thousand golfers were surveyed and 70 percent said they did not warm up. Only 3.8 percent said that they warmed up on every occasion. The reasons for not warming up included the perception that they did not need to warm up; they didn't have enough time; and they couldn't be bothered." He adds, "Studies have shown that golfers' performances will sig-

Christopher doing a few warm-up excercises.

nificantly improve by undertaking a golf-specific warm-up program compared with not performing the warm-up. Also, golfers who reported not warming up on a regular basis were more likely to have reported a golfing injury in the previous twelve months than those reporting frequent warm-up participation."

No statistics exist on how many of those golfers walked off holding their backs and complaining about their scores. And speaking of walking, in addition to doing a golf-specific warm-up, walking may also aid performance in golf. By increasing your movement through walking or jogging, you may improve your reaction times. Bottom line: if you perform a golf-specific warm-up (which has been shown to increase clubhead speed) and walk the course, your chances of playing better golf increase.

In addition, recent research has shown that you can actually coax the brain to grow new nerve cells with cardiovascular exercise. Now, walking a round of golf may not be considered cardiovascular exercise for some, but the more your blood is pumping throughout your body, the more oxygen your body is going to get. And the more oxygen your cells get, the more efficiently they will work.

Christopher doing a few warm-up stretches.

"I CAN CHANGE, BABY"

Now that you are warmed up, you need to pick an exercise program that will work for you—meaning one you will continue to do for more than a week, and one that will help improve your game.

So what are some things to look for in a golf fitness training program?

- You need to pick a program that is consistent and time efficient. Consistency over quantity produces your desired outcome, which is gain in a short period of time.

- Also, pick a program that is safe—you don't want to get injured doing your fitness program; it must be helping you to prevent injury.

- And the workout must be performed! Although this may sound obvious, if you do not train consistently, you must not embark on a program. Find a workout you enjoy, stick to it, then change it every four to eight weeks to keep things varied and interesting. Find one that focuses on general overall strength and flexibility.

According to Ziobro, who was part of the strength and conditioning staff during the University of Kentucky's NCAA Basketball Championship runs in 1996 and 1998, "A workout only gets you stronger if the overload of the muscle is greater than what the muscle is exposed to on a regular basis. Therefore, finding the right workout is like finding the right diet or the right putting style—it's got to work for you."

Interestingly enough, strength training can improve many things other than your strength.

- Strength training, when performed through its full range of motion, improves your flexibility.

- If done with little rest, proper strength training improves cardiovascular endurance (more important in golf than you realize and especially important in speed golf!).

- Strength training with proper overload (fatiguing the muscle to the point of failure) improves your speed and control.

- Strength training releases endorphins, which help reduce stress for an improved mental state.

- Strength training with proper overload puts muscles into a state of recovery, which increases metabolism, thus affecting your diet and weight.

Here are a few guidelines for your strength training:

1. Control is paramount. Whether it is one or fifty sets, dumbbells or machines, eight reps or a hundred, the repetition must be controlled. Momentum doesn't stress

the muscle, which must happen in order for the fibers to be overloaded. When a weight is moved quickly, momentum is created and tension is reduced to almost zero. Momentum also greatly increases the risk for injury. So it is better if you do at least a seven-second repetition, with two seconds to raise the weight, a one-second pause, and four seconds to lower the weight. A rep can be performed slower than this, but not any faster. The golden rule of strength training: you control the weight, the weight never controls you.

2. Ideally, you want to do one set per exercise, consisting of six to fifteen slowly performed repetitions executed to the point of muscular fatigue, meaning you will not be able to perform the last rep (that's how I'm feeling on the fifteenth tee in a round of speed golf, wishing I were on the eighteenth green already). The muscle must be exhausted to the point where you could not perform another rep even if you tried. To achieve overload, in the next workout you will strive to increase the number of reps to fifteen; when you can do fifteen controlled reps, it's time to increase the weight by one to five pounds.

3. To increase your cardiac response, don't rest between exercises. Your strength workout will take twenty to forty-five minutes, leaving you more time to make golf swings (if you can still lift your arms). It's the main reason I play speed golf at all: I don't have time for five-and-a-half-hour rounds of golf—got other things to do.

4. The best order for your strength training is:

   - Legs
   - Back
   - Chest
   - Shoulders

Christopher demonstrating a few strength exercises with free weights and on machines.

Christopher demonstrating strength-training exercises.

- Arms
- Forearms
- Abs/low back

5. Workouts need to be performed one to three times a week.

If all you did for your fitness was a constructive strength work-out as just outlined, you would derive a wide range of benefits in all aspects of your overall fitness. Speed golf does much of the same for me. I get my eighteen holes of truly golf-specific practice in, with all of the challenges (mental, management, etc.), and I get my cardio workout done in a parklike setting. What a deal!

Let's touch briefly on the two other physical components of overall fitness, cardiovascular and flexibility training, and how they influence and affect us in a round of golf.

Cardio training is obviously huge when it comes to speed golf, but an improved cardio level benefits the traditional golfer as well. You fatigue less and hit better shots under the late-hole pressures of a round. Some things to consider when working on your heart muscle include:

- You must enjoy the exercise, so run outside if you like to be outdoors, or use an exercise bike if you like to read while cardio training. Walking, StairMaster, elliptical: do what-ever you enjoy and will work on consistently.

- The golden rule of cardio is, you must keep moving for twenty minutes. "Continually strive to improve," Ziobro emphasizes. "For example, walk for twenty minutes for two weeks, then increase to twenty-two minutes after two weeks, or run for forty minutes and add a ten-second sprint at the nineteen- and thirty-nine-minute marks. After two weeks, increase the sprint to fifteen seconds. The heart is a muscle, and thus must continue to be challenged."

When I don't have a golf course handy to specifically practice speed golf, I will often do interval running to simulate what my body is experiencing while running between shots. So, to simulate a typical par four, I may run hard for 275 yards (a drive), stop for approximately ten seconds (to catch my breath and select my club), run for another 150 yards or so (a typical iron shot), stop for thirty seconds (time on and around the green), then sprint 50 to a 100 yards (to simulate going to the next tee box). Although I'm not physically hitting shots, I am in my mind (remember, the subconscious doesn't know the difference between real and imagined), and I am training my body for what I will experience in a round of speed golf.

"BEND ME, SHAPE ME, ANY WAY YOU WANT ME"

To state the obvious: swinging a golf club requires flexibility. Swinging a club well requires a great deal of flexibility in both the muscles and joints. Muscular tightness and joint stiffness contribute to bad golf swings and injuries; both can be avoided if you spend a few minutes every day stretching your old, tight body. "Muscles get tight from not being pulled to their available tension length, and joints get stiff from a lack of isolated motion," Ziobro points out. To do it right, you must:

- Hold a stretch for twenty seconds and perform two or three sets. Recent studies have shown that there is no added benefit to holding a stretch for longer than thirty seconds, but that adding additional repetitions will increase the benefit of the stretch.

- A stretch must not be painful. Do not force a stretch, as this can result in injury. Allow your range of motion to improve over a long period of time, say six to twelve months. You did not get tight overnight, nor will you turn into a gymnast in one or two sessions.

Pictured here are some muscle stretches that are important for injury prevention, for overall health, and for help in the performance of your desired golf swing. Set aside five minutes a day and do them two to five times a week.

(1) Doorway/pec strength. (2) Hamstring stretch. (3) Hip flexor stretch.
(4) Press up/lower-back mobilizer. (5) Rotational mid-back mobilizer.
(6) Wrist flexor/golfer's elbow stretch.

WHAT YOU CAN LEARN FROM SPEED GOLF

If ever athleticism was needed in a round of golf, it would be when you are playing eighteen holes in forty-five minutes while carrying your own bag (albeit with only six clubs) and trying to shoot under par. That's what I'm doing during a round of speed golf.

My chosen form of golf requires explosive movements, sprinting, endurance, and mental clarity while my heart rate is going up and down like an elevator. Because of that, I have to train in a way that will have maximum effect. I have a good strengthening and interval-running program, and I practice on the golf course while my heart rate is up toward the top 10 to 15 percent of its target range.

The good news is, because I train so hard, a leisurely round of regular golf is no more stressful than sitting around the house watching a football game. Being in good shape means that a round of regular golf puts little or no pressure on my body. It's a bit like Lance Armstrong going out for a five-mile bike ride with a bunch of kids; he barely breaks a sweat, just as I can walk thirty-six holes of golf without fatiguing any part of my body.

You might not become a speed golfer, but being in better shape will definitely improve your game, and your attitude. So why not give it a try?

TEN

O O O

"Journey to the Center of the Mind"

This entire book has been devoted to teaching you how to build your most natural, optimal golf swing and game—the one that works best for you—while eliminating all the game-killing swing thoughts that clutter the mind and bog down your game. Play faster, ponder your swing less, get out of your own way, and you will play better: that is the message I will pound home to my students as long as I am able to teach this game.

But I'm not naïve enough to tell you to blank out all thoughts while you're on the golf course. You are not a machine, you are not in a coma, and you are not brain-dead, which means you cannot possibly clear your mind of all thoughts. Even when you sleep, you don't clear your mind. Dreams are the brain's way of hitting the reset button. Neurological research has proven that thoughts continue even when you're sound asleep; you cannot turn off your brain any more than you can will your heart to stop and start. Plus, you need the analytical and rationalizing conscious part before and after your swing—just not during.

Neurobiologists have begun to observe some interesting patterns. Before people consciously think about doing anything—

whether it is wave at a friend, open a book, or make a golf swing—the brain regions needed to perform the activity are already ablaze. The notion that any of us is the "decider" may simply be a happy and perhaps necessary illusion.

According to Bernard Gasquet, a mental preparation coach for the French National Olympic Teams from 1982 to 2000, "We must never count on the ability to master a motion *during* its execution. This is a formidable illusion that will make you lose time—and even more important, make you lose confidence in yourself."

To understand this paradox better, consider the task of an Olympic-caliber marksman. For many years now, in the realm of shooting, it has been universally recognized that the actual firing of the gun must *surprise* the shooter. What is the significance of this statement? Gasquet explains: "Quite simply, that the central motor act of the shooter—to pull the trigger—cannot be controlled, mastered, regulated or modified voluntarily in its crucial phase. At a certain critical point, will (mental desire) and consciousness must take a backseat and allow the unconscious automatism to take the reins. Otherwise, the conscious part will interfere with and infect the motion instead of perfecting it." Thus, the conscious is surprised by what the subconscious has done.

So the question becomes: if you eliminate conscious swing thoughts during your motion, what do you put in their place? If you can't turn off the brain, what do you think about instead of your swing?

The simple answer is: anything.

Remember when David Duval shot 59 in the Bob Hope Chrysler Classic? It was a record performance, one that not only put Duval in elite company (only two other players in history, Al Geiberger and Chip Beck, have broken 60 in PGA Tour events) but led to a win and helped propel Duval to the number-one ranking in the world. So what was he thinking about as he walked up the eighteenth fairway needing an eagle on the par five to break 60? "My caddie and I were talking about how they got that car out in the middle of the lake," Duval said.

Sure enough, mere moments before he drained an eighteen-foot putt to make history, Duval was thinking about the Chrysler sitting on a platform in the pond next to the green. How did they get that car out there? I'm sure that's what would occupy *your* mind as you walked up the final fairway to thunderous applause.

To reiterate, each part of your brain has its role: consciousness prepares the shot and analyzes the result, the subconscious executes it. If these roles are reversed, you will fail. Will and consciousness create the program in the brain and fire it up, and then the cerebral baton must be passed to another part of the brain responsible for executing the chosen program. Our motions/acts, programmed and arranged in a conscious and voluntary manner, are actually executed in an automatic fashion. Why does it work this way? Quite simply because, although thought is capable of imagining an act at dazzling speeds, the control, the command, and the modification *during* the material execution of the act demand a response time between the thought and the motor apparatus (the body) that is superior to our physiological capabilities.

Conscious thought must be reserved for those times *away from* the actual moments of execution. It must be relegated to the following times:

- *Before* the motion
- *After* the motion

At these two points in time, the conscious has all the time in the world, and hence the ability to alter the selected program.

Arnold Palmer, without question the nicest superstar athlete in history, not only fed off his "army" of supporters, he used the gallery to occupy his mind between shots. When it was his turn to play, Arnold would focus on the shot at hand, visualizing exactly what he wanted the ball to do and executing the shot with a level of intensity seldom seen outside the Tour ropes. But in between shots, Arnold was always winking at the girls, chatting with the guys, patting friends on the back, shaking hands, and introducing himself to strangers. This served two functions: it allowed Arnold to engage socially with the people who were supporting him—a function that came as naturally to him as eating and breathing—and it distracted his mind from the zillion swing thoughts that plague most amateurs.

My students do much the same without realizing it. Often the best shots I see while giving a lesson are the ones the player hits while we're in the middle of a conversation. We're talking about one point or another, maybe even arguing about something— usually something non-golf-related and humorous—and the student hits a couple of shots during the discussion that are the best of the day. This is not because of my supernatural teaching skills. The student swings better because the mind is occupied with something other than the normal swing thoughts, and the subconscious is reacting to the situation and environment. The mere act of talking "quiets" the conscious mind and allows the subconscious—with all its experience, brilliance, and savvy—to perform the task at hand.

Now, unless you are a rock star or a celebrity, you don't have an Arnold Palmer–type gallery following you around the course and offering a distraction, but you probably have playing partners to talk with. Even if you aren't much of a chatterbox, you can keep your mind occupied in a number of different ways, eliminating the bad thoughts and replacing them with something positive and good for your game.

"NO DOUBT"

Tommy Lasorda tells a great story about his early days managing in baseball. It was a close game, and his pitcher was throwing it well. When a power hitter came to the plate, Tommy called a time-out and walked to the mound to chat with his pitcher. His only words of advice were "Don't throw it low and outside." Of course, low and outside is exactly where the pitcher threw it, and the batter corked one out of the park. "That was the last time I ever told anybody what not to do," Lasorda said.

The mind can never process a negative. So when you say to yourself, "Don't hit it left," the last thought that stays in your mind is "Hit it left." That is exactly what happens. And more often than not, "right" isn't any better than left. If you say to yourself, "Don't miss it," you can bet the farm it's not going in.

"You never hear a Tour player say, 'I know I can't make this,' " says Brad Faxon. "A good Tour player believes he can make every putt, no matter how long or how difficult, and he's trying to make it. You might hear a guy say later that he was just trying to get it close, but that's BS. We're trying to make everything."

Doubt in golf is end-stage terminal. Doubt has destroyed entire civilizations, never mind golf swings. And if you are—after my endless harping—having doubts about the value of your swing thoughts, consider the following: if you have to *think about* how to swing the club, you must doubt your ability to do so correctly. You don't think about how to walk, talk, or tie your shoes. And you are very successful in performing these skills. Doubt in the mind of the golfer is pure arsenic, and it's as common as pine trees in Augusta. Common negative, doubt-filled, swing-killing thoughts include:

- Don't hit it in the water.

- Don't leave it in the bunker.

- Don't top it.

- Don't come over the top.

- Don't leave it short.

- Don't pull it.

- Don't slice it.

- Don't hook it out of bounds.

- And whatever you do, don't three-putt.

Those thoughts are precursors for all of the preceding outcomes occurring as surely as thunder follows lightning.

Anytime you tell yourself not to do something, it is reinforcing a negative thought and increasing the likelihood that the thing you fear most will occur. Instead of dwelling on what you don't want to do and where you don't want to go, you need to replay a positive result over and over in your mind until you convince yourself that it is the only possible outcome.

The best way to do this is to focus solely on the task at hand—getting the ball from point A to point B—and to the exclusion of everything else. And the best way to do that is to not give yourself enough time to second-guess. When I'm playing speed golf, the only thing I'm focused on is what the approximate distance will be for the next shot, which club I might be using, and where I want the next shot to end up. Talk about "staying in the present." If I hit a lousy shot, I have no time to pout, ponder, or fix what may have gone wrong. I'm immediately heading for the next shot at hand and have left the previous one behind. Last I checked, H. G. Wells and his time machine are nowhere to be found on the golf course, so I have to play the game "in the now," unconcerned with the past or future.

Speaking of the now, consider the following regarding fear and staying in the present from bestselling author Eckhart Tolle from *The Power of Now*:

> A large portion of psychological fear is about something that *might* happen, not about something that is happening now. *You* are in the here and now, while your mind is in the future. This creates an anxiety gap. If you are identified with your mind and have strayed out of the "now," that anxiety gap will be your constant companion. You can always cope with the present moment, but you cannot cope with something that is only a mind projection—you cannot cope with the future.

There have been plenty of occasions when I've run past water hazards without ever seeing them. I never see the out-of-bounds stakes, even as I am sprinting past them, just as you probably don't focus on the power poles on the side of the road as you are driving past them. If you stared at those poles, you would find yourself driving off the shoulder, just as staring at the water or the woods will lead to hitting your golf ball right where you were looking.

Because I am running, I don't have time to focus on the bad parts of the golf course. I have to calculate distance and visualize the shot I want to play in the few seconds it takes to run to the ball. This is another example of playing better by playing faster. When you're driving your car, you don't have time to think about all the obstacles whizzing past you on the left and right. You focus on the road ahead without realizing you're doing it. When you only have time to think about where and how you want the ball to fly—not all the spots where you don't want it to go—you end up close to your target. Even when you don't have the luxury (or ability) to play in an hour or less, you can still focus solely on the shot you want to hit, not where your right elbow and left shoulder need to be at the top of the backswing. There is no reason for you to stare at the ball, stare at the green, and stare at all the trouble off to the sides and in between. If you are waiting on the people in your group or on the group ahead of you, look at the trees; smell the flowers; find figures in the clouds; do whatever you can to distract yourself until it is your time to play. Then you should focus only on the shot you want to hit, commit yourself, and get on with it.

Heed the words of Henry David Thoreau: "The question is not what you look at, but what you see."

"HEY, GET RHYTHM WHEN YOU GET THE BLUES"

I waited almost until the end to throw in Johnny Cash lyrics. The point of this great song is that getting a little rhythm cheers you up when you're feeling blue. And golf will make you blue. You're going to make bogeys and doubles; you're going to hit bad shots and miss putts you think you should make. But as any decent psychologist will tell you, the sooner you can put the past behind you and focus all your energy on the present, the quicker you will recover from previous mistakes.

The best way to get off the emotional free fall is to rely on your natural pace and rhythm. If you hit a bad shot or have a bad hole, you should immediately fall back into your normal routine—walking at your normal pace, choosing your club the way you always do, talking, and swinging with the same rhythm that you have throughout the day. And please, don't forget to breathe. It's a natural form of meditation. Most people start their rounds to the cadence of Pachelbel's "Canon in D," and after a couple of bogeys they are marching to the staccato beat of Ted Nugent. The walk gets quicker, the grip gets tighter, the swing gets shorter, and the scores go higher, all because you let your emotions take you out of your natural rhythm and pace and put you on a runaway train to Bogeyville. Control your emotions or your emotions will control you.

I, of course, can't let myself get down or depressed when I make a lousy swing, because I have to run to my next shot. The rhythm of running between shots keeps me on an even keel no matter how well or how poorly I'm swinging the golf club. You don't have that luxury in regular golf, but you can keep your wits about you by tapping your toes, clicking your heels, singing a song, doing a few simple stretches, visualizing, and hearing the beat of a metronome, anything to force yourself out of the blues by getting back into your normal rhythm.

"I COULD DREAM SOMEBODY ELSE"

Everybody has doubts. You start feeling a little out of sorts, a little self-conscious about your game, and before you know it, you're doubting your ability to hit shots you could normally pull off a hundred times at midnight. Even the best in the business fall into that trap.

To overcome these doubts, a lot of good players trick their minds into believing they are somebody else. Anytime Jack Nicklaus felt his swing slipping away, he would imagine that he was Sam Snead. He tried to walk like Snead and wave to the crowd like Snead; as he set up to swing, he even imagined himself standing outside his own body watching Snead execute the shot.

More recently, Adam Scott does the same thing, imagining that he is his hero, Greg Norman, on those occasions when he can't find his own rhythm. This is a wonderful way to take yourself out the equation and thus eliminate the anxiety that kills so many potentially good rounds. If Nicklaus is your hero, imagine you are Jack. He wouldn't worry about hitting it in the water on the par three; he wouldn't flinch at the tee shot on the narrow par four; and he wouldn't waver over the must-make putt to win the match. If you can trick your mind into believing that Jack has taken over your body and you are merely a rooting spectator, you will get over your doubt and hit more good shots. Call it imitating, mimicking, or an out-of-body experience, the act of role playing helps to fill your mind and body with pictures, motion, and feel—and thus eliminate nagging swing thoughts.

"WHAT ARE YOU AFRAID OF?"

The lyrics in this heading come from a band called Virus Nine, which answers the question "What are you afraid of?" I'm afraid of anyone who listens to a band called Virus Nine.

But the analogous point of the lyrics is that fear on the golf course is a silly emotion, one you should chastise yourself for feeling every time it creeps under your skin. What the heck are you afraid of? Professional bull riders have every right to feel a twinge of fear in their game: they climb on the backs of two-thousand-pound bovines that will do whatever it takes to throw them off and step on them. An NFL quarterback has the biggest, meanest, and strongest athletes on the planet wanting to break him in half on every play. Fear is a very rational emotion in that circumstance. But you are on the golf course, for goodness' sake! Nobody is trying to kill you.

Whenever you feel fear, think about people who are in real jeopardy at that very moment. Someone in the world is having his life threatened while you are enjoying a game. Keep that in mind the next time you start shaking over a three-foot putt. What will be the consequences if you miss it? Will your family disown you? Will there be world peace if you make it? A little perspective goes a long way in golf. The reality is, trying and caring too much will not improve your performance—it will more often hamper it.

WHAT YOU CAN LEARN FROM SPEED GOLF

The longer you take over a shot, the more time you give that demon child known as doubt to creep into your mind. Look at a putt from nine different angles, and doubt will become your best friend. I rarely experience doubt or fear when I'm on the golf course, because I don't have time for either. You might not be able to control the time it takes you to play a round—especially if you are playing in the middle of the day with several groups in front of you—but you can control the amount of time you spend focused on the shot and all the things that can go wrong with it.

Try playing a round without ever taking a practice swing and without looking at your ball until it is your time to hit. Don't squat down to read a putt, and certainly don't look at a putt from both sides of the hole. When it's your turn to play, look at the hole, look at your ball, look at the ground in between, and hit it. You can spend the rest of the round smelling the flowers and enjoying the wonderful scenery and your playing partners. You will be stunned by how much better you play.

○ ○ ○

ELEVEN

"I Should Have Known Better"

Ben Hogan said that if he showed up at a major championship with two swing thoughts, he would probably finish in the top ten; if he showed up with one swing thought, he would win the tournament; and if he showed up with none, he stood a good chance of setting the tournament scoring record. After a round of 68 at the vaunted Seminole Golf Club in the early fifties, Hogan said, "I never know *why* I hit the ball well. I just know when I'm doing it." I don't expect you to break any U.S. Open records, but I do hope you will remember that anecdote when your mind wanders back to the endless array of swing thoughts that have never worked in the past and will only make you play worse in the future.

When it comes to managing your golf game to shoot lower scores, "shoulds" and "coulds" have to go. In fact, I've tried to eliminate them whenever and wherever possible in this book. "Should" is always someone else talking, not you. It's the Golf Channel, one of the major golf publications, the people you play with, or perhaps even your local golf professional. Thinking you should be able to achieve or do something is abiding by someone else's expectations. Last I checked, you were the one swinging the club and playing the game.

My heartfelt and professional insight: stop "shoulding" on yourself; set your own goals and expectations according to your own strengths, weaknesses, and capabilities; and don't worry about what anyone else thinks.

"Coulds" aren't much more beneficial than shoulds when it comes to thinking your way around the golf course. Turn the "could" into a "can"—a definitive positive statement about what you are planning on accomplishing. A "could" once again reeks of doubt, one of the most destructive thoughts in the mind. More shots end up in bad spots because of poor decisions than poor swings. Managing the golf course is first about making the correct choice of the shot to be played, then executing it. Here are a few examples of "shoulds," "coulds," and other typical poor golf-course-management decisions that lead to high scores—and, more important, some positive alternative options.

- *"Reachable par five . . . wide landing area off the tee . . . I should reach back for a little extra on this one."*

How often do you hit a good shot when that thought enters your head? If it's more often than "never," you are in the minority. Plus, how many times are you going to reach a 600-yard par five in two? If you reach a 510-yard hole in two shots, you are a heck of a good player. Why reach back for a few extra yards on a hole where your distance doesn't mean anything? You could hit a 5-wood off the tee and a 5-iron from the fairway, and probably be much closer to the green and in much better position to make par or birdie than if you tried to reach back for a few extra yards.

- *"I could play this game if I could just hit it ten yards farther."*

I want you to play a game with yourself the next time you are out messing around on the course. Hit the ball as far as you can on every hole, and if you miss the fairway, pick up the ball and carry it back to the middle of the fairway . . . but move it back twenty yards. If you hit it out of bounds or in a hazard, bring it back to the middle, but back it up twenty paces: no penalty.

Then keep that scorecard on your desk or nightstand as a reminder of what's possible when you hit it shorter and straighter every time. For my students who believe that adding distance is the end-all to lower scores, I will often play a round of golf with them where I never hit a shot more than 200 yards: I won't even have a club in my bag that will go any farther. After they've seen me play in even par or better, the message becomes a bit clearer.

- *"Pin's tucked close to the edge. I should hit a flop shot onto the fringe so I can stop it close."*

The title of my next book is going to be *Flop Shots Are for Dummies.* Unless you are practicing the short game two hours a day, forget about trying to hit a big flop shot to a closely cut pin. And if you are practicing that shot two hours a day, you have way too much time on your hands, unless you are playing golf for a living.

There is nothing wrong with playing away from the pin and giving yourself a decent chance at making bogey, and an outside chance at a par, as long as you take double bogey or higher out of the equation. As big a thump as that might be to your ego, it will be an even bigger hammer blow when you chunk three pitches in a row and walk off the par four with an eight or nine on the card.

- *"Never up, never in."*

If you think running a putt five feet by the hole is better than leaving it six inches short, I want to play you for your pension. Sure, to repeat an old, bad joke, 99 percent of all putts left short don't go in, but it's tough to three-putt when you leave your first putt an inch short of the hole. Plus, last time I checked, the putt that finishes the optimal seventeen inches beyond the hole and the one that ends up an inch or two short have one thing in common: neither of them went in. The real issue I have with focusing on leaving the putt seventeen inches by the hole if you miss is that you are thinking about missing. Why would you ever do that?

I'll take the player who leaves a few putts short, but never has a second putt longer than a couple of feet. We'll win most of the games we play.

- *"I'm more than 200 yards from the hole, so I should hit all I've got and try to get it somewhere near the green."*

Is buried in the front bunker better than being 75 yards away in the middle of the fairway with a wedge in your hands? And how close do you hit that 20- to 50-yard pitch from the high rough— or anywhere, for that matter—really?

Too many people look at the yardage and pull the club regardless of the conditions or what the likely outcome of the shot will be. Considering your "leave," that is, the spot from where you want to play next, will help you select the right club and hit the shot that has the highest potential for success.

Longish par fives are the best example of this, with the 3-wood second shot being the poorest choice. Keep that 3-wood in the bag unless:

- An average shot will get you green-high and there are no nasty hazards around the putting surface.
- You have an extremely good lie. Long clubs with thirteen to fifteen degrees of loft do not perform well from so-so or bad lies.

- *"Doggone it; I hit it left on this hole every time."*

In this situation, you have multiple options:

- Line up farther to the right and stand there until you get it figured out.

- Aim it left and curve the ball away from where you hit it every time.

- Use a completely different club.

- What are you so afraid of *on the right?* There may be something you are so trying to avoid down the right side that you always hit it left. Focus on where you want to go, not on where you don't want to go. A lot of golf course architects angle tees so that they face the trouble in an attempt to see if you will be lulled into lining up with the tee box instead of to your target. If you have a hole where you miss it in the same spot most of the time, check your alignment first, and then stand out on the tee with a bag full of balls, if necessary, until you can hit the ball in play.

- *"I should play aggressively, trying to attack every pin."*

I bet you make a lot of high numbers, too. One of the best golf lessons I've ever heard came from five-time British Open champion Peter Thompson, who said that when he was winning all those opens, he never carried a pin sheet, because he didn't care where the pins were. "If I hit it in the middle of every green, I'm going to be pretty close on six or seven holes, and on the others I'll never have more than a twenty-footer," Thompson said.

I've held tournaments where there were no pins in the holes to prove that point. Invariably, participants in those events played better when they didn't know where the holes were cut. Same is true with nighttime tournaments played with those glow-in-the-dark golf balls. You know, candles as tee markers, a fluorescent, glowing stick hanging from the flag—and nothing else. You can't see any of the spots you don't want to go (trees, hazards, etc.), only ball, target, and where to start from. Most players shoot lower scores than in broad daylight.

- *"I'm only 150 yards out; I should be able to hit an 8-iron."*

Just because you caught a flier out of the rough one day with a twenty-knot tailwind and hit the ball 150 yards with an 8-iron does not mean that this is the club of choice every time you have that distance. I've played links courses in Scotland and Ireland where I've hit wedges 200 yards and good solid drivers 170, depending on the wind, rain, and other conditions. If you become locked in to thinking a club goes a certain distance no matter what, you are never going to hit the ball close to the hole on a consistent basis.

- *"I hit that same tree every time I play this hole."*

Well, hit a different club! If your normal shot pattern with a driver puts you in trouble—next to a tree or in a bunker, whatever—hit a 5-wood off the tee, so that you are short of whatever obstacle is in your way. You aren't going to change your swing for one hole, and if you do, you're probably going to be in more trouble than if you simply took a different club and hit the shot you know. There is no rule that says you have to hit a driver on every long hole. Hit the club that gives you the best chance of making a decent score and eliminates the trouble from your mind. Or you could pull a Moe Norman. When told a certain par four was a driver-and-a-9-iron hole, Moe used those clubs—only backward. He teed off with his 9-iron, then hit a driver onto the green.

- *"I should chip rather than putt."*

Arnold Palmer once said that 90 percent of his bad putts wound up closer than a majority of his good chips. That is true for most players. If you are in the fringe and don't have any holes or bumps or sprinkler heads to go over or any longish grass to negotiate, you will get the ball closer to the hole with a putter than with any of your chipping clubs. Some old Scottish insight: never hit the ball in the air unless you have to.

- *"Clubs shouldn't make that much of a difference."*

A friend of mine—a low-handicap amateur who played college golf and still competes in local amateur events—told me that when he was in college twenty-five years ago, he averaged 260 yards off the tee, which was considered long back then. Now, with a new 460-cc driver, high-tech graphite shaft, and super distance golf ball, he flies it 280. "That's not because I'm older and fatter," he says.

In the long-running debate over whether it is the arrow or the Indian, the arrows are winning. Equipment technology is so good these days that the right clubs can, indeed, shave several shots off your score. You still have to make good golf swings—no manufacturer has come up with a self-hitter—but the new stuff certainly makes the game a lot easier.

- *"Lessons have never done me much good."*

Professional golf instruction is like any other professional advice: it is only as good as the recipient's willingness to follow it. "A teacher is only as good as his student's ability to work and learn," Ben Hogan once said. Lessons do not take the place of practice; they make practice worthwhile. We are not faith healers. I can't lay hands on you on the driving range and force the evil shanking spirits to come out. As is often the case, everyone is looking for the magic pill, but as a teacher—or "learning facilitator," as I prefer—I can only open the door. You have to walk through yourself. All I, or any other instructor, can do is share knowledge, experience, and insight, giving you the guidance, the tools, the games, the equipment, and the plan to become a better golfer.

The rest is up to you. Golf instruction can only be useful if it is put into regular practice.

Finally, the moment we've all been waiting for, in David Letterman style, from number twelve to number one, my "Dirty

Dozen," those lecherous and confounding swing thoughts that are always going to blow your scores to smithereens and leave you shaking your head and cursing this blasted game.

12. Keep your left heel down in the backswing.

Why would you be thinking about part of your foot when the gist of the game is to get the ball from point A to point B? Depending on your overall strength and flexibility, and the type of shot you may be hitting, your left heel may need to rise slightly for you to make a decent backswing, so let it do its thing, and focus on what you're trying to do with the ball.

11. Finish high.

This sounds like the title of a new Cheech and Chong movie. Finishing high was trendy back in the seventies, and probably will be again someday soon. Your finish will be a reflection of your golf swing and the shot to be played (high, medium, low, left to right, right to left), nothing more.

10. Rotate.

Rotate what and how much? Your tires? A hugely vague swing thought—the worst sort. If your focus here is on your hips in the downswing. Remember, from the top of the backswing to impact takes one-fifth of one second. Good luck thinking about anything.

9. Stay behind the ball.

As opposed to being in front of it? Yes, with a driver, most good players' heads are several inches behind the ball at impact. Trying to keep too much of your body behind the ball can result in the clubhead striking the planet Earth before it strikes the ball. Oops.

8. Don't slide.

Deadly "don't" number one. *Sliding* is a hugely misunderstood term. The lower body (normally the "sliding" culprit) will react properly if you picture and feel the motion of throwing a ball: bracing the back leg going back—no sliding or kicking out so that the weight would end up on the outside of the foot—then stepping forward to initiate the forward motion.

7. Don't move your head.

Deadly "don't" number two. If you are trying to build a powerless, inefficient golf swing that causes injury, abide by this swing thought. Try throwing a ball without moving your head. No chance. The head has its own natural pivot and motion, which is largely dependent on eye dominance. You're already trying to get "out of your head," so don't be thinking about it!

6. Slow backswing.

There's nothing good about a slow backswing—unless you are trying to develop terrible tempo. A child's swing doesn't move back slowly; it swings back with pace and freedom. Let your club do the same.

5. Shift your weight.

Do you think about shifting your weight when you throw a ball? Of course not. Weight shift in the backswing is created by the motion of the upper torso and head (the heaviest part of your body), not your legs. On the downswing, a lateral move forward with the lower body gets things going, just like the step you take to hit a pitch.

4. Turn.

Right up there with "rotate" in terms of vagueness. Turn what and how much? Your shoulders? To what degree and on what plane? I see as much overturning and incorrect turning as I do anything else. You are hitting something forward (the ball) that is on the ground, with a stick (the club). Set your body up in the optimal position for you, and trust your mind/body system to figure out the turning part.

3. Accelerate the clubhead/don't decelerate.

Absolute poison for all short shots. There's only one thing worse than deceleration—that's overacceleration. Yes, you want the clubhead to be accelerating as it is going through the ball, just as a children's swing accelerates near the ground—naturally, due to the laws of physics. When the clubhead is decelerating at the ball, it's because it has run into the ground first. That usually is caused by overacceleration (often the result of a short, slow backswing), by you getting in the way of the natural swing of the club (helping—pushing, pulling, steering, guiding, etc.), and by screwing with the laws of gravity and momentum.

2. Keep your left arm straight.

Ouch! Literally. This thought will lead to elbow tendonitis, rigid backswings, and weak, slicing shots. Most PGA Tour players have a slight amount of bend in their left arms in the backswing. Lee Westwood has his left arm bent throughout the swing. In the follow-through, let the left forearm rotate and fold, and the sore elbows and slices will go away.

1. Keep your head down.

Why? To avoid topping the ball? You don't hold the club with your head; you hold it with your hands. Trying to keep your head down frequently causes the club to come in to the ball too high, as it forces the arms to bend and the body to stop moving. And as Jackie Burke Jr. pointed out so well, "Most things in the wild that keep their heads down eventually get eaten."

Yoga teaches that your body follows your eyes, so if you keep your head—and hence eyes—"down" after your shot, you will probably find yourself in a semiparalyzed position. Keep your eye on the ball after it takes off, and allow your head and body to follow.

Epilogue

○ ○ ○

"Get Up and Enjoy Yourself"

I don't know anything about your golf game. The downside of writing a golf book is the impersonal nature of it: I've never seen you swing or play. I haven't seen how you react to adversity, and I have no idea if you break par, break clubs, or feel great when you break a hundred. But I know that the swing thoughts that have ground your game to a snail's pace are keeping you from learning and finding the swing that works for you, and holding you back from reaching your full potential as a golfer.

"Today we know that approaches to learning based on self-development are more efficient than following someone's 'how-to' directions," says Michael Hebron, a PGA Master Professional and 1991 National PGA Teacher of the Year. "Our brain did not learn how to use our hand and arm when we learned to brush our teeth—it learned what to do with the toothbrush," he adds.

The how-to teaching that is so prevalent in much of today's golf-swing instruction actually interferes with the brain's ability to encode personal information, which is so vital to learning and performing the skill of hitting a golf ball. Following how-to directions is a form of outsourcing, whereas individuals best learn and develop when simply interacting with the environment and responding to the task at hand—in this instance, hitting a ball to a target. Picturing and feeling what you want to do with the clubface, clubhead, and shaft just prior to, at, and just after impact, to produce the result (flight of the ball) is much more productive than thinking about *how* to do it. From the result, your mind/body system can begin to adjust as needed, accordingly. Remember, the genius of the human race is our ability to adapt and adjust; that's how we've survived for millions of years. We were designed to do, observe, and adjust, each of us in a way that best suits our needs and capabilities.

I hope this book has given you the tools to eliminate the unnecessary clutter from your mind and helped you see that learning, like playing great music, is an individual pursuit, and that is best mastered less consciously.

According to psychologist Frederick Perls, "We all need to get out of our conscious minds and into our senses. Learning is discovery." When you think about it, everything in our world that is now real was first an image. A golf swing, a table, an automobile, etc., were initially someone's image. Therefore, picturing what we want the ball to do and how the club and body must present themselves at impact to produce the desired result are the most important and natural aspects of learning an efficient golf swing. In addition, research from cognitive science points out that all the mechanics of learning (regulatory feedback, conceptual construction, and synthesis) are nonconscious. "Trying to consciously achieve makes golfers less aware and is therefore distracting to performing a motor skill," Perls points out. "Learning requires much more than memorization, repetition, and rote. Following someone else's how-to directions, doing drills, or copying an expert model are acts void of imagination, curiosity, and the problem-solving skills that cause learning to take hold," he adds. Therefore, optimum performance is allowed to happen, not caused.

There is one thought, though—actually, let's call it a "notion," in keeping with our thought-bashing theme—that I want you to remember. It is the most important golf-related notion of all, the one you must keep in mind every time you pull into the parking lot of your golf club, get your clubs out of the car, and head toward the first tee; the one that will help you hit the ball more solidly, make more putts, shoot lower scores, and win more matches; and the one that will improve every aspect of your golf game and make you a lot more popular among your playing part- ners. That one notion is: it's a game, enjoy it. It's not a science, and, much like life, it's not fair. You must always expect the unex- pected, and enjoy the adventure.

You might not become the player you dreamed you would be, but if you keep that one thought in mind, you will become the best player your talent and ability will allow.

Acknowledgments

I never know quite where to start on the thank-you list, so I will begin with Mark Reiter, Steve Eubanks, and the folks at *Golf Digest* for making this project happen. A privilege to be given this opportunity—thank you.

Since the theme of this book is how to stay out of your own way to learn and improve your golf by playing faster and less consciously, I want to thank some people who have helped me to convey this message to you, the readers.

Golfwise, I want to thank my first coach, the individual who showed me this wonderfully wacky game firsthand, Bruce Alexander. As my fifth-grade basketball coach, Bruce introduced me to golf and all its intricacies—and I've been hooked ever since. Along the way, my golfing education has been influenced by so many players, teachers, and others, the list would be endless. Special thanks to Paul Runyan, Jim McLean, and Jerry Mowlds, in addition to my other colleagues that I have shared the lesson tee with for the past eight years at Pumpkin Ridge Golf Club, Bruce Furman and Verne Perry. No ink on these pages without you.

Playing faster and less consciously came to me unsuspectingly in the form of speed golf. I must thank my original speed-golf partner in crime, Tim Scott, for joining me in picking up the pace on the golf course—it's been a fun run, and still is. Although I wasn't much of a runner as a kid, growing up in the track-and-field hotbed of Eugene, Oregon, I must have a bit of it in my blood. I saw Pre and Alberto run—and Bowerman coach—and I wish to thank those men and all my friends and colleagues at Nike and Nike Golf who have influenced and supported me over the years.

I would never have had a chance to do any of this without the support of my parents—thanks, Mom and Dad. All the times you carted me around, to and from the golf course, while encouraging me with my golf and other dreams. Lastly, thanks to the thousands of people who have by happenstance crossed my life's path in large or small contexts, and who, albeit quite unconsciously to me, have had a huge influence on what I've tried to communicate in this book. We all know that golf is but a microcosm of life. The challenges presented to us on the golf course are simply preparing us for the moments when it really matters—during the game of life.

Index

Page numbers in *italics* refer to photographs.